101 LESSONS LEARNED FROM HELPING MILITARY MEMBERS AND VETERANS ACHIEVE MEANINGFUL, LUCRATIVE POST-SERVICE CAREERS

Eric "Doc" Wright, PhD
Editor-in-Chief

Cathy Miclat
Editor

Contributing Authors

"JB"
US Army

Russ Barnes
US Air Force

Jeremy Burdick
US Air Force

Steven B. Crane
US Marine Corps

Paul DeJarnette
US Air Force

Garrik Dennis
US Army

Reid Denson
US Army

Joey
Eisenzimmer
US Marine Corps

Dave Esra
US Army
Reserve

Joshua Frank
US Army

Heide Gabriella
US Navy

Clint
Gershenson
US Army

Mark Giles
US Air Force

Mark Hannah
US Marine Corps

Kaylin Haywood
US Air Force

Philip Hicks
US Air Force

Craig A. Jones
US Marine Corps

Daniel
Kaminske
US Air Force

Mike Klingshirn
US Air Force

Kevin A. Knight
US Army
Reserve

Matthew
Kolakowski
US Army

Michael
LeJeune
US Army

Timothy
McCardle
US Marine Corps

James McCulley
US Army

Raphael
Montgomery
US Army

Misty Moreno
US Air Force

James Onder
US Air Force

Eric Paddock
US Air Force

Patrick Pressior
Canadian Forces

Joe Pusz
Veteran
Advocate

Ray K. Ragan
US Army
Reserve

Adam Reed
US Navy

Nick Roberge
US Marine Corps

Stuart Smith
US Army

Bruce
Townshend
US Army
Reserve

Robert Tyson
US Army

Carlos V.
Ulibarri
US Army

Craig
Washburn
US Navy

Dana L. White
US Air Force
Reserve

This book is dedicated to all those brave men and women serving in the defense of their Nation and fellow citizens; some of whom stepped forward here to share their lessons learned with you, to help you achieve a meaningful, lucrative post-service intra or entrepreneur career. Thank you!

Contents

Foreword

It wasn't that long ago when I was sitting at my desk in Quantico, Virginia and faced the dilemma to either accept orders for an unaccompanied overseas assignment or decide that it was time for me to pass on the torch after twenty-five years of service to the Marine Corps. Although I was frustrated with the career monitor at the time, I had to take a step back and realize that I didn't want my family to either start again in a new location or be without their husband/father as they continued to move on with their lives without me being around.

This led to submitting my retirement papers and receiving the perfectly folded American flag from my Marines as they presented it to me after performing "Old Glory". That moment not only caused me to reflect on the many years that I had the privilege of serving this great nation, but also the journey that was in front of me as I began my transition from the military. I am sure in some form or fashion; you can relate to this story because the decisions that I made at that point have led to experiences that I would have never encountered otherwise.

One thing all veterans have in common is that regardless of your branch of service nothing can explain the brotherhood and deep bonds that are created among the veteran community. As I was getting out, I did not realize how complex the process would be and was told that "finding a job is the hardest job you will ever have", which could not be closer to the truth.

I was unaware of the invaluable resources that were available to me and even if I were aware, I would not have known where to start. There were not any lessons learned that I could draw from nor was there a "one stop shop" that laid out a roadmap for people transitioning out of the military.

Over the course of my post-service career, I have been fortunate enough to engage with many veterans who were determined to lay out a path and pay it forward to those coming behind them. However, Eric "Doc" Wright is an individual that stands out from the crowd. After serving his time in the Navy and ultimately becoming a highly successful entrepreneur and keynote speaker, I have grown to know and trust Doc as someone who practices what he preaches.

He continuously educates himself by understanding industry best practices, conducting extensive market research, building relationships with corporate leaders (like himself), and ultimately sharing that information in a practical, yet deliberate way. So, when he approached me to write the Foreword for this book I jumped at the opportunity because this isn't just a book, but rather a compilation of lessons learned from fellow veterans willing to share what it is like "on the other side of the wire" and provide insights on how to negotiate many of the pitfalls that will be experienced along the way.

This is what makes veterans unique and so valuable to corporate America. We have all encountered adversity and strife within our lives and for those who have served, we have been conditioned to persevere in the face of it all. This book provides not only an outlook on transition hurdles, but also relays important "Mission Tips" that can help you navigate those obstacles and overcome what lies ahead. It is a "must read" for anyone that has served in the military (to include military spouses and dependents) because we all experience our own version of the transition and need to understand practical ways to negotiate our path through the "fog of war".

Marcus "Ohley" Ohlenforst
Military Talent Strategist for a Fortune 500 Company

Preface

Like many other military veterans, my transition from military service to the civilian workforce was long, arduous, and dark. Twelve years long. And in fact, so arduous and dark at one point, it almost killed me. Well, my own hand almost did.

However, in the twenty-plus years since, I have worked in all sectors of our economy, succeeding in organizations of all sizes and stages, at university, and as a founder of a couple LLCs (Vets2PM, Vet Stone, and Double U Holdings) and one 501(c)3, the Veteran Project Manager Mentor Alliance ("VPMMA").

For the last several years, I and my teammates at Vets2PM and my fellow executive board members at the VPMMA have helped thousands of transitioning military service members and veterans achieve and sustain meaningful, lucrative post-service professional careers in the civilian workforce.

This book is a collection of 101 lessons: (1) collected from 39 of those thousands of transitioned brothers and sisters in arms; and (2) my teams assisting them. This format makes it easy to start and stop reading it. Easy to comprehend. And tailored; you use only those lessons learned applicable to you.

Thank you for serving and for reading this book, thank you to those brothers and sisters that helped us write it, and thank you to my extraordinary teams at Vets2PM and VPMMA that support our transitioning military service members and veterans. I hope you enjoy it! The information contained herein has been distilled from the toil, blood, sweat, trials, and tears of thousands of your brothers and sisters slogging through their own transitions. I look forward to hearing from you and serving you in any way I can. You can find my contact information in the back of this book.

Doc
Indialantic, Florida
February 2020

Lesson Learned ("LL") #1: Your first job out of uniform probably will not be your last!

Eric "Doc" Wright, US Navy ("USN") & US Army National Guard ("USARNG")

This means that you are not looking for the job or career you are going to retire from next. You are instead looking for a gig that provides enough sense of purpose, enough meaning, and enough money in a geographical location you want to be in to lighten the transition burden. Heck, the average civilian will change jobs an average of seven times over their career, which spans an average of four fields![1]

So, take some pressure off yourself! The head space and timing you will create for yourself will give you time, resources, energy, and room to explore what you want to do in the civilian workforce, i.e. the CIVDIV, when you 'grow up'. Which may not be the first thing you land right out of service.

---

[1] http://careers-advice-online.com/career-change-statistics.html#:~:text=The%20average%20person%20will%20change,or%20jobs%20every%2012%20months.

LL #2: Steppingstones?

Jeremy Burdick, US Air Force ("USAF")

Do not confuse LL #1 with building a steppingstone mentality! Hiring managers can smell, "I just want to get my foot in the door" all day long. In fact, this very attitude cost me a lucrative position in a major company. I believe during the interview I asked, "are there advancement opportunities in this position?" The hiring manager heard, I do not want to be a part of their team, I just want to advance to the next one.

You see, the interview is not an assessment of your resume, trust me they can read, but rather, an assessment of your ability to fit into their culture, team, and organization. Unlike the military, they get to choose who they share workspace with. Show them you are a great candidate to hangout, work hard, and play with! A simple change in your perspective is what I am suggesting.

For example, instead of just trying to land a job so you can step up to the next bigger thing, treat the opportunity as a chance to learn how the organization works, the amazing skills you will bring to your team in a new capacity, and the experience you will earn by joining a civilian organization.

LL #3: "Get good with LinkedIn"!

Eric "Doc" Wright, USN & USARNG

Transitioning service members will hear "get really good with LinkedIn" ad nauseum in transition classes, from mentors, and on LinkedIn. However, instead of just giving you generic "get really good with LinkedIn" advice, I will give you specifics proven effective in thousands of transitioning service member and veteran profiles!

To me, "get really good with LinkedIn" means two specific things. First, it means dial your LinkedIn profile in. Second, it means use the platform to find organizations you would like to work at. Let's take a quick look at each.

Dialing in your profile means:
1. Provide a header image related to the industry/feeling you would like to create in the viewer.
2. Have a professional-looking picture that is close-up enough we can see your warm smile and sparking eyes. That's right, no Ray Bans on!

3. Under your name is not your default professional title that LinkedIn sticks there, but a meaningful, descriptive, concise tagline that is your Value Proposition Statement (VPS). The character count on this VPS is as few as possible. Your VPS is about you, but not for you. Tell them who you are, what you can do for them, and how it benefits them. For example, my 163-character long VPS reads "Veteran | Business Philosopher | Founder | Author | Speaker helping veterans, managers, and owners achieve meaningful, lucrative post-service professional careers!"

4. Create a custom, personal URL for your profile. My profile's URL is https://www.linkedin.com/in/docwright2012.

5. Be sure to write your About section, i.e. your professional summary, in an engaging conversational manner, i.e. first-person. It feels more like a conversation, your story. "I am X, who helps Y, so they achieve Z!" It is a more detailed version of your VPS, and opens a story line in their minds that they now want to close; what would our success look like with this person on our team? Your value and memorability just shot way up!

The second part of "get really good with LinkedIn" means learn to use the platform to find organizations you would like to work at. Here is how:

1. Think about the values that are meaningful to you, jot them down. Search companies on LinkedIn, and then those companies Websites, that have those values.
2. Think about things you like to do and do not like to do, or things you liked about your favorite roles/billets and things you didn't like about your least favorite roles/billets. Use these keywords in company/job description searches.
3. Think about a salary number you are happy with, as well as which benefits, you would like.
4. Connect with folks that work at the short list of companies now that fit you, your values, and your needs. Start conversations with them about does their company live its values? Does the company value their customers and employees? What is the culture and climate like inside their walls? What types of projects do they do? What things were they asked about during their interview? The key is developing a genuine relationship and dialogue.

This drill helps in three ways. First, you now know whether you would really like to work there or not. Second, you know which questions to ask in your interview, and always ask some! I know HR officials and executives that will not hire a great candidate if they do not ask meaningful questions. Third, you demonstrate concern about things regarding the company, in a language familiar to them. People like people like themselves, and you seem like them, so you must enjoy similar things!

LL #4: Build "purposeful" relationships – organize for quality over quantity

Eric "Doc" Wright, USN & USARNG

Throughout your lifetime you have probably heard the saying "you are who you hang around". This can have either a negative or positive spin to it depending on the context of the situation. When selecting who you connect with during your transition, your goal should be to build "purposeful" relationships, not "check the box" on having 500+ connections on your LinkedIn profile.

This leads into the importance of choosing quality over quantity. If the end goal is to have relationships that are meaningful and fulfilling, then it is important for you to identify ways on how you can help them, help you, help them.

Identify groups of connections.

For example, my network consists of business owners, business students, veterans, human resources ("HR") professionals, executives, project managers, and event organizers. My knowledge, experience, goods, and services can help them, which also means they can help me, which means our networks can help each other! When we post content and engage with each other in professional conversations, it is helpful to both parties!

MISSION TIPS:

- Building "purposeful" relationships takes time and focus, but it is worth the investment. Spend the time.
- Design a networking strategy that develops a solid foundation that can be nurtured.
- Add a couple meaningful connections a week to your network.
- Like and Comment on your network connections' content when moved to.

LL #5: Ask for help!

Eric "Doc" Wright, USN & USARNG

In general, many veterans are not comfortable asking for help. However, everything in the CIVDIV is about time and money. If you proverbially break something, someone else has to clean it up, and that means there is time and money associated with the clean-up. These are expenses, i.e. costs incurred to make and sell goods or services, which are subtracted from the revenue, which is all the sales of goods and services we achieved during the period. Clean-up reduces profitability, which is the net difference between revenue minus expenses.

Therefore, if you increase expenses, you decrease profitability. The problem here is not the mistake, it is that it could have been avoided. Avoid it. Ask for help! Your organization has experts in each business area paid to do it; to help. They would rather it gets done right the first time, than gets done heroically, but wrong. Hundreds of executives and human resource professionals recognize the importance of this topic and have told me they want us to ask for help.

LL #6: Become comfortable talking about you and your contributions!

Eric "Doc" Wright, USN/USARNG

Much like we veterans are not typically very good at asking for help, we are also generally not very good at talking about ourselves. It seems individualistic, ego-maniacal, and violates our sense of integrity to take credit for what others did, and we are always surrounded by team members.

However, in the CIVDIV, bragging about one's self and one's contributions is commonplace in many organizations. One primary reason that hiring managers and bosses provide is "I can't hire you/promote you if I don't know what you individually contributed", and "your individual contributions have to be greater than the salary amount I am paying you".

So, one common tactic is to talk like a STAR! Present good news items about you and your performance in terms of the Situation, Task, Actions, and Results. "This was happening (situation), and we needed this to happen (task), so I led, directed, did these things (actions), which produced 1, 2, 3, n results". This method highlights your contributions, in context of how they helped the organization. It serves both purposes.

Remember that it is not really about you, but how your experience, knowledge, talents, and capabilities allowed you to influence outcomes. Managers know there were others involved probably, but we will discuss that with them in their interviews and performance reviews. Where they talk about themselves.

LL #7: Maintain a positive attitude!

Jeremy Burdick, USAF

Transition experiences are different for everyone, but there are several similarities I have found after talking with hundreds, maybe thousands of Veterans. We all hear of or know someone who received a six-figure salary offer while they were still on terminal leave (you know, the last few days you burn just before getting back into the phone booth and trading the cape for a briefcase).

However, it is not the majority of transitioning veterans that receive these offers, I can assure you. Imagine if I told you, change is scary, fear of the unknown is a real thing, and uncertainty always equals risk, most of you would say, "I already know that" and you would be right! The military transition is difficult because of the aforementioned reasons and you were part of a distinct sub-culture (uniforms, comradery, shared pain), then it was or will be pulled away like a magician pulling a tablecloth. The change is so fast, only the saltshaker fell, and you now have to move out like nothing happened. Fast-forward, you are in corporate America, the rules have changed, the clothes have changed, and ranks are hidden.

Now is the time to employ your military bearing and I do not mean suffer in stoic silence; on the contrary, make a choice to be positive, be grateful, and be thankful. We were fortunate to learn sacrifice is a real thing and people must fight for freedom. Positivity can be found in small victories, you submitted one more resume, you can still complete your fitness test, you kept your lights on for one more month. Gratefulness is remembering what others are doing right now to keep you free and you were a part of it, they now stand on your shoulders. Thankfulness is an outward expression to someone who helped you along the way. Praise it forward.

LL #8: Establish your personal criteria!

Marcus "Ohley" Ohlenforst, US Marine Corps ("USMC")

Transitioning, which as a veteran we know better than anyone, is a difficult time for not only us, but also our families. Throughout our time in service we have always been told what our next duty assignment was going to be, what our next job was going to be, and who our next boss is going to be. News flash – in the CIVDIV that does not exist! WHAT?? Do you mean to tell me that I can actually "choose" where I want to live, how I want to work, and who I want to work for? YES!

However, keep in mind that although this road (in many cases) may have never been travelled and you might or might not know what will be around the corner, what you need to be confident in is that as long as you continue moving forward then you are heading in the right direction.

It is understood that not everyone is married or has a family when they transition, but for the context of establishing a personal criterion it mostly applies to anyone regardless of their situation.

Some of the most common variables when transitioning is geographical location, types of industries in the local/regional area, access to educational opportunities, etc. When considering all of the variables relative to your transition, it is a good idea to weigh these in a manner that establishes a criterion.

For example, if I spent the past XX years of my military career commuting to and from my job, then maybe (now that I have a choice) one segment of my criteria is to search for companies that are within 30 minutes from my home. Another example is if my goal is to get a degree, certification, license, etc. and there are not any colleges/universities near me, then maybe another segment of my criteria might be to choose online programs that are accredited through a university. At the end of the day, just know that you have options and as long as you invest the time, then you are on the way to finding your next career where you will not only be happy, but also comfortable in the decision you made for you and your family.

MISSION TIPS:
- Establish key indicators for your personal criteria and use the bracketing process to map out your goals.
- Identifying your personal criteria is like starting to paint on an empty canvas 1) Categorize your career goals, 2) Design the parameters, and 3) Develop a plan.

LL #9: Transition is your opportunity...set your sights!

Russ Barnes, USAF

Whether you have served 3 years or 30 years...when the time comes to separate from the military, it need not be a leap into the unknown. It is, in fact, your opportunity to shape the rest of your entire life. It's a matter of perspective. If you see your military service as "ending" then the image of your future is that of standing on the edge of a cliff looking into an abyss, filling you with feelings of the fear of falling. If you see your military service as "extending" then the image of your future is that of a vast uncharted landscape that you can shape to your desire, filling you with the potential and possibilities of prosperity.

When I looked into my future as I approached my retirement following 27 years of active service, I set my sights on entrepreneurship. I wanted to control my ability to take action on my own decisions. I wanted to control my schedule and my time. I wanted to receive reward based on my hard work, ingenuity, and resourcefulness. This was how I described freedom...and freedom was what I wanted.

Transition is your opportunity to craft your path and it starts with deciding what you want…and why you want it. I committed to my intention and ten years later, I am here. I have control over my ability to take action on my own decisions. I have control over my schedule and my time, I receive reward based on my hard work, ingenuity, and resourcefulness. I have the freedom I wanted.

It was not easy, but it is worth the effort. You will not want what I wanted. Perhaps you want a job with a reputable company that offers career progression. Perhaps you want to play golf. It's *your* decision. I recommend taking as much time as you need to reflect on how you want to live the rest of your life and seize the moment to set your own course. Transition is your opportunity.

LL #10: Yep, the CIVDIV has a doctrine too!

Eric "Doc" Wright, USN & USARNG

You need to know it! The civilians do, even if only subconsciously. They recognize it and operate comfortably in it because while you were off defending our collective lives and liberties for X years, they were working in it! Realize that the civilian workforce, what I call the CIVDIV, has a doctrine too! Just like your service branch! I'll explain it here, so you have heard it once. It will be key in helping you talk about your unique experience in a dialect they can relate to, and thus understand.

Managers in the CIVDIV carry out this doctrine by 1. Planning, to include creating associated objectives and performance standards; 2. Organizing the resources to carry out the plan; 3. Leading the human resources executing the plan; and 4. Controlling performance to plan, tweaking both as we go so that we hit the objectives to standard. This involves decision-making and behavior around shared values and norms, with fiduciary responsibility as the ultimate measurement. Do we steward our resources successfully and make the company more profitable...?

If what we are doing is not operational, i.e. it is a temporary project or program, we simply add an initiating function and a closing function. The initiating function describes what we're going to do so we can get agreement and authority to do it. And the closing function ensures we pay all of the bills, close all the contracts, and file all of the paperwork to ensure compliance.

Additionally, we do all of this in congruence with the organization's structure, policies, procedures, and applicable operating and HR laws. These organizational components make up the CIVDIV doctrine, values, decision-making method, culture, structure, and fiduciary responsibility, i.e. get the mission done.

This means that when you talk about yourself at networking events, or on social media, or in your resumes and interviews, talk about your military experience across all four to six functions so they see your full experience. Otherwise, if you only speak in leadership, you could receive baffling rejection letters of "unqualified" or "underqualified" because you have failed to impress upon them you are the full meal deal, not the dollar choice. That is a gut punch; I know, I have received them!

MISSION TIPS:

- Consider earning the Institute of Certified Professional Managers' Certified Manager ("CM") certificate to validate your military management and leadership experience into the CIVDIV context.[2]

---

[2] https://www.icpm.biz/index.php/icpm_site/certified-manager

LL #11: Get a four-year degree!

Eric "Doc" Wright, USN & USARNG

It is the price of admission to a great job today. Plus, if you don't, you will leave a lot of dollars on the table in terms of lost earning potential. Just know that in addition to all of the other pros and cons of pursuing your degree, like time and effort sink, you may experience connecting with some of your fellow students and professors a bit difficult. They do not have your experience. And most of their perceptions about you and military service are inaccurate. So, a couple mission tips below...

MISSION TIPS:
- Ensure the school is accredited.
- Consider high demand fields.
- Find other veteran students or join a student veteran peer group; Student Veterans of America comes to mind.[3]
- Find professor and student mentors.

---

[3] https://studentveterans.org/

LL #12: "I don't think we are in Kansas anymore Toto"!

Philip Hicks, USAF

What are your expectations after being in the military? The military puts skilled people in leadership positions under highly stressful (sometimes combat) situations. Most leaders of the companies and organizations you are entering have extensive experience in the company, market, and business. You can expect to probably not start out at the top of an organization. But you can successfully work your way to the top by employing the skills developed during your military career.

Continue to use the skills that made your military career a success and develop new skills. Broaden your leadership skills beyond the autocratic directing method of the military because the civilian marketplace looks for consensus building for implementation of plans of action.

One definition of "persona" from Merriam Webster's Dictionary is "an individual's social facade or front that especially in the analytic psychology of **C. G. Jung** reflects the role in life the individual is playing". Your military persona as "Lieutenant Colonel," "Major," "Command Sergeant Major," "Chief Master Sergeant," etc. no longer exists. While respected by military outsiders, you are no longer that individual.

You are a singular person providing skills and abilities to an organization. What value can you provide to the company? How are you improving the bottom line? The transition from an identified military member to a civilian can be the most trying.

I hope and pray everyone has established a strong moral and ethical base for the transition because this will help you identify the person you want to be after you retire. I pray your faith, voluntary efforts, and family will help you define who you will be in the future.

Final notes...remember you are not alone in this journey. Remember to reach out to friends, family, and your support systems for help during your transition. The resources available to military members during transition are many, but they are useless if not accessed.[4]

---

[4] https://www.linkedin.com/pulse/20141024143510-168102092-my-military-retirement-journey/

LL #13: Stay connected so you stay out of your head!

Eric "Doc" Wright, USN & USARNG

A difficult aspect of the transition to civilian life is the feeling of being alone. As a dear friend of mine, Max Rodgers, US Navy veteran, once put it, "the reality is you will never serve with the caliber of people you once did again". The bond of tribe will probably never again be as strong, as palpable as it once was.

The only reason I have achieved it again is because of my team at Vets2PM. But it took eighteen years, several pounds of flesh, an ounce of my soul, lots of thinning and graying hairs, in a company and culture I had to found.

For many civilians though, the thoughts are "keep my head down, take of myself, worry about me getting ahead" and "just meet the standard". Mediocrity is an acceptable standard in many organizations. You have to be proactive and seek out like-minded individuals, form tight bonds with them, and just accept your network is probably now a couple dozen, instead of your entire field, or branch, or year group.

LL #14: This salary is for this job!

Eric "Doc" Wright, USN & USARNG

Many veterans and their families are concerned about salaries and benefits. So, two points here. First, when negotiating salaries, know what you are worth and what the going rate for what you are interviewing for is. Second, do not let the employer bring your retirement pay into it, if you have some.

In fact, let them know that since you are talking about what you will do for them, that actually has no bearing on your current negotiation. I mean, they don't ask their civilian employees about previous 401Ks or benefits accrued at previous employers during their interviews! Shame!

LL #15: "Free" and "Non-profit" should not be your only considerations.

Eric "Doc" Wright, USN & USARNG

Hear that banging? That is me angrily climbing onto my soap box! And I am mad! I am so sick of hearing transition advocates write off legitimate individuals and companies because they do not give their goods and services to veterans for "free", and that any organization that isn't "non-profit" is not worth a veteran using.

I hate to break two things to these folks. First, you often get what you pay for. Want a free resume? Sure, it is only your career and livelihood on the line! Want a free LinkedIn make-over? Sure, it is only a potentially powerful lifeline to a great post-service gig!

Want some training? Sure, take the free stuff that either allows you to bang your mouse through a static PowerPoint slide deck or is provided by folks that are not practitioners in their fields. If they were, they would have a price tag associated with their expertise!

My point is simply this: the need for education and training post-transition will continue, and there is a shelf life on how long you are a 'transitioning veteran'. At some point, you'll have to begin footing your own bill to train. Just be diligent about the organizations you choose, and specific about why you're choosing them, ensuring they meet your needs.

Second, 'non-profit' is just a tax status! It does not mean the goods and services the non-profit provides are any better, or any worse, than those provided by for-profit corporations. Money in the bank account is either profits or donations, but they are both dollars necessary to keep the doors open and the lights on.

I know. I have founded both; multiple LLCs and one 501(c)3.

If "free" government and non-profit programs are the silver bullet, how come the transition process is still so busted after all of the decades they have had to fix it? How come survey after survey of veterans consistently reveal gaps? Remember point one? Yeah, often times, you get what you pay for…

MISSION TIP:

- Pay close attention to the details for "Free" or "Non-Profit" organizations when considering career support options.

- Do not write all non-profits and all "free" things off, that would be as ridiculous and as reckless as writing off all for-profits and paid services. Just do your diligence and figure out what meets your needs best, regardless of the provider's tax status.

- Always ask "what's in this for this person or organization?" The answer may surprise you. At the bottom of their Websites you may notice an "LLC" or "Inc.". Those do not stand for "non-profit", they stand for Limited Liability Company and Incorporation, i.e. companies that make money, i.e. profits, to survive. Which means they don't survive on donations. Which means they are either overtly or covertly advertising themselves as non-profits, or letting the market think that they are, both of which should raise suspicion based on unscrupulous behavior...

LL #16: Underemployment is a thing?

Eric "Doc" Wright, USN & USARNG

Regardless of the survey and the source, many veterans consistently report they feel underemployed.[5] In fact, Military-Transition.org's digital multi-era, multi-branch survey reveals that only 52% of the respondents felt their first CIVDIV job aligned with their existing skills, and only 51% liked or like their first CIVDIV job.[6]

This means they are in jobs that do not provide them with purpose, meaning, challenge, or the pay they think they deserve. However, you do not have to stay in that position now. Leaving one job for another better one, however you define "better", is acceptable in the CIVDIV. Switching jobs and careers every two to four years is commonplace, and it does not ding your commitment or integrity to do so. It is the way it is on this side of the wire.

---

[5]   https://recruitmilitary.com/employers/resource/941-underemployment-remains-an-issue-for-americas-veterans

[6] https://www.military-transition.org/dashboard.html

LL #17: Spouse employment.

Eric "Doc" Wright, USN & USARNG

If veteran unemployment and underemployment is a thing, you'd better believe it is even worse for military spouses! According to the US Department of Defense ("USDoD"), it is 24%[7]. Wow!

There are many factors, but here's a few low-hanging ones: there are multiple workforce entry and exits on the resume, there are career and salary challenges, there are PCSes, and there are home front challenges such as daycare, finances, and loneliness, just to name a few.

In this light, entrepreneurship can be a sound way to go for many military spouses. The gig economy has created many opportunities to start and run a home-based business. Recruiter, virtual assistant, notary, bookkeeper, and resume writer are some examples that come to mind.

---

[7]

https://www.defense.gov/Newsroom/Releases/Release/Article/2091431/dod-releases-military-spouse-licensure-report/#:~:text=Military%20spouses%20face%20a%2024,higher%20than%20the%20general%20population.

In fact, at my LLC, Vets2PM, we help military spouses establish their own home-based businesses. See, one of the services we provide to our transitioning service members and veterans in our training program is resumes. We have automated tools, processes, and personal phone calls that help us craft what the service member or veteran did into what they are capable of and want to do now, producing a forward-looking resume focused on providing value to the hiring organization. That means we write thousands of resumes per year! Which means a lot of resume writing!

So, we help military spouses set up home-based businesses, and then provide them with the work! This helps not only the military spouse, but also helps us help our military service members and veterans, and our great Nation's economy too. It keeps them in the resume game from a work history perspective, provides them confidence, mobility, satisfaction, and financial fortitude.

As an additional aside, we also hire veteran student alumni to teach for us. Again, we show them the basics of business, help them set up a shop, and then we push work to them. Heck, we even hire our best of the best sometimes! In fact, we were a Department of Labor 2019 HIRE Vets Gold Award Winner in the small business category for our veteran hiring initiatives! All of our hires in 2019 were veterans! And, we're in the running again this year in 2020! Boom! Money where the mouth is! Walking the talk!

LL #18: Paint a new end-state.

Eric "Doc" Wright, USN & USARNG

Regardless of branch, rank, service length, or military occupation, there are two watershed days every military veteran shares; the day we went from civilian to Soldier, Sailor, Airman, or Marine, and the day we went from Soldier, Sailor, Airman, or Marine to veteran. In between was lots of structure. If you wanted to be an E5, E9, CW03, or O6, you knew what to do in order to make that end-state come to fruition, and you could do it.

However, the day you transition out of uniform, that is gone. It is just you and your future. And you are just John. Or Jane. So, just like in the military, paint what you think is your new end-state, so you have something to start moving towards. You may get blown off course, but you also may find the island you end on is just as nice as the one you were navigating towards!

MISSION TIPS:
- Use LinkedIn to build a network of people in positions, companies, or places you admire.

- Find several mentors. The Veteran Project Manager Mentor Alliance[8], Veterati[9], and American Corporate Partners[10] come to mind.

- List professional key words that resonate with you and look for job descriptions with them in it. Capture those requirements. Use these to help you build your professional development plan.

---

[8] www.thevpmma.org

[9] www.veterati.com

[10] www.acp-usa.org

LL #19: "Don't speak military!"

Eric "Doc" Wright, USN & USARNG

During your transition, you will hear "don't speak military!" during every transition class and from every transition guru out there. Ad nauseum! And I get it. Very few civilians will understand what you're saying.

However, what chafes me is that very rarely do they suggest *what* to speak! And if they do, at best it's usually the same tired, outdated techniques we've been kicking around for decades. So, you're left confused, and silenced.

And as an additional reality, most professions you will go into will have their own lexicon of terms, jargon, and idioms. It's similar, you're simply trading one lexicon for another. That's the key then, learn what to speak instead, and then translate your military experience into that target language.

So, here is how to identify what to speak, how to speak it, and just as importantly, demonstrate fluency speaking it! I have done this with thousands of veterans. It works. And it not only makes you familiar to the folks hiring and promoting you, it increases your stock price too! Watch!

The CIVDIV has a doctrine, (see CIVDIV Doctrine Too on page 34) and an associated lexicon, or language, associated with it. So, we have CIVDIV doctrine and words like "P&L Statement", "director", "general manager", and "control". We add to this "A/P" and "A/R" for accounting let's say. To help you figure out how to talk about what you did in a language and dialect understandable by civilian hiring managers and peers, do this...

1. Pick an in-demand credential that a certain industry values, like PMP, Scrum, and SAFe for project management, Sec+ and CISSP for cyber security jobs, APHR, SPHR, and SHRM for human resources professionals, CM for general management, etc.

2. Then go to their source documents, i.e. their bodies of knowledge (BoK) and credential handbooks, and translate your military experience into those terms and concepts on your resume, LinkedIn profile, and speech so that you sound like the professionals fluent in that target language.

3. Then apply, study, and obtain the industry credential to validate your resume's experience.

For example, for me personally, project management made a great post-service career. It is full of responsibility, accountability, stewardship, team development, leadership, camaraderie, stakeholder influence, results orientation, and critical thinking and decision-making to solve organizational problems to make them better, or faster, or cheaper. Plus, it has a unique, universally understood lexicon, i.e. collection of terms, clustered around temporary, unique works, i.e. missions, which allowed me to translate my military experience into experience understood and valued by corporate America. I hold a PMP and ACP from Project Management Institute[11], a CPD from the Institute of Project Management[12], and CSM and CSPO from Scrum Alliance.[13]

---

[11] www.pmi.org

[12] https://institute.pm/about-certification/

[13] https://www.scrumalliance.org/get-certified

This has worked for not only me, but for thousands of other veterans turned project managers, i.e. Vets2PM. I have seen infantry NCOs and Officers talk about patrols and firefights in terms of project management and win the interview! I have seen first shirts and top sergeants talk about running units in terms of people, process, benefits, and talent management and land meaningful, lucrative HR roles! I have worked with Navy submarine drivers and data analysts in learning how to talk Sec+, CISSP and AWS (Amazon Web Services), and then watched employers fight to hire them, providing them with high five/low six-digit salaries, and sometimes, even signing bonuses!

LL #20: Stu's Secret!

Stuart "Stu" Smith, USA

I'm going to tell you THE SECRET to a successful transition from military service, but only if you PROMISE TO TELL EVERYONE. You see, those of us who have successfully transitioned know the secret because it works; it's the only thing that does work, and yet we are told to do things in our transition that are the exact opposite of the secret. So, if you promise to tell everyone, I'll share the secret.

"You might as well do the opposite of the advice you're getting; you'd have better luck finding a job". That's exactly what I was thinking as I hung up the phone with Steve, a career Army NCO who was in a transition program and was leaving the service in a month. Steve was excited about the future, so I didn't want to rain on his parade, but he was listening to people he trusted to help him with his transition, and they were giving him bad advice. It was the typical spiel – "work on your resume, take the first job offered and above all else, despite your 20+ years of experience and leadership, be willing to start at the bottom". It was also the opposite of the secret.

Just then I remembered the words of an old platoon sergeant who said, "motivation rules the day", so keeping Steve motivated while explaining that he was getting poor advice was going to be challenging. I decided it was time to tell him that the advice he was getting was not the way to find the job he wanted and deserved. I decided to share the secret with him.

The secret was revealed to me during my own military transition. You see, I was fortunate when I left the Army. I went to work for the Washington State Department of Veterans Affairs as a Training Specialist the Monday after I ETS'd. From BDUs to suit and tie over a weekend. I did not write a resume. The job was a perfect match of my military skills and experience, and it was a job of significance and importance. I loved going to work every day and it was the job that ignited my passion for helping my fellow Veterans. Since leaving the Army in 1992, I've helped many Veterans transition successfully based largely on my own experience and sharing the secret with them.

The next time I talked to Steve I knew I had to get him to recognize what he was doing, and the advice he was getting, was not working – without dampening his spirits. We started the conversation with a quick "sit-rep" (situation report). "How are things going Steve?" I asked. "Man, lots of good stuff" he replied. "I spent hours on my resume over the weekend and everyone I know reviewed it and gave me advice. I've applied for 15 jobs online with some really good companies. On top of that, my father-in-law said I could always move back and work with him". "Wow!" I thought. If this is good stuff, I would hate to think about his search going poorly! Lots of busy work, loaded with more bad advice and most importantly – not a single face-to-face meeting with someone with the power and interest to hire Steve.

There it is. The secret. Simple, straightforward. And when you learn it and know how to do it well, your transition will be a success. In fact, once you learn it and do it all the time, most things you pursue after the military will be a success. If you missed it, I'll repeat it. The secret is finding someone who is willing and able to help you. Whether it is coaching and supporting you in your transition or finding those who want to hire you, it's all about working to find those who can help. See, I told you the secret was simple.

Truth be told, it's not a secret at all. I know, I know, it's not what they told you, it's not the career search advice you got in the transition program. But the facts are clear; 70-80% of all jobs are never posted (Forbes) and the number one way to discover open jobs is through referrals (LinkedIn). So if you are taking advice that is focused on writing the perfect resume, applying for every job opening and taking a job that does not match your skills, experience and most importantly, your passion – you are getting the wrong advice.

So, it was time to leverage Steve's motivation and help him get in front of those who could help him. And by the way, that's not always "HR". In fact, human resource people don't "hire you". Think about it. Their job is to find you, qualify and screen you, and then put you in front of the person who is going to hire you. Something else they never tell you as they are encouraging you to find the organizations' HR leader and send them your resume.

I asked Steve, "What are you passionate about"? He started with an almost rehearsed response – an "elevator pitch" as they call it. I stopped him right there – "No, Steve what are you passionate about?" I asked him a series of questions to get him thinking and on the right track. "On a weekend morning what would you get up early to do? What do you love to do in your free time? What do you talk to your friends about over drinks and dinner? What's YOUR passion, Steve?"

He was stumped for a second. Then he said, "I love to ride motorcycles; you know, dirt bikes". Now we got something. Steve's new job was now within reach. Don't jump ahead, I was not going to tell him to send his resume to Kawasaki and let them know he wanted to be the new sales managers since he rides on the weekend. There's more to the secret, so please follow along.

In an earlier conversation, Steve and I had talked about LinkedIn and the importance of a good LinkedIn profile. At the time, LinkedIn was not as popular as it is now, but you could see the potential of having a searchable "resume" online 24/7. But that's not the power of LinkedIn; connections are the power of LinkedIn.

We talked about "how to" identify people; connect with them; and schedule time to have a conversation. That's it. A conversation. Not an "informational interview" or any other term to describe the "I'm searching for a job and I need your help" ambush conversation. Just a conversation to get to know the other person and ask them questions about what they liked to do and what they were interested in and passionate about. You see there is great power in listening to others, connecting them with people you know, and being interested in their success.

"Steve, here is what I want you to do. I want you to find three people who are into off-road motorcycling and have a conversation with them. You have ten days to contact them, schedule a conversation with them, and then get back together with me to talk about what you found out". Steve was listening. I encouraged him to use LinkedIn to search out professionals in the field and then find a connection – either someone who knew them and who would be willing to introduce him, an affinity connection such as their veteran status, or any other information to use as an introduction.

At first, he was uncertain this would work, but I went on to explain and role-played a conversation with him so he would feel comfortable contacting someone he did not know.

Steve found three people. A salesman who had been in the Army, in fact he had served in a unit Steve had also been assigned to; a writer for a motorcycle magazine who had just been recognized for his writing; and a repair shop owner who one of Steve's motorcycle buddy's knew. Perfect. Three candidates, one with an affinity association, one with a common connection and someone who would be willing to talk about their recent success – easy conversations.

Now all Steve had to do was decide what he was going to say on the call or write in the email to schedule the conversation. I encouraged him to let them know a little about himself, but quickly move the conversation to what they were most interested in and passionate about. He called the salesman and let him know he was transitioning and wondered if he would be willing to give some advice based on his own transition and in return Steve would "pay it forward" to others who were leaving the service.

He let the writer know he was also an avid rider and asked if there were other stories he was interested in writing because Steve would be happy to help introduce him to the riders he knew.

He asked the repair shop owner if there were any unique repair problems or situations that were challenging to solve because Steve had ridden all kinds of bikes and he would be willing to share what he knew. The final "close" was "besides, it will get you away from the office to talk about motorcycles and I'll buy lunch". Motivated as always and mission focused, Steve emailed me at the end of the day to let me know all three conversations were scheduled.

Day ten couldn't wait. Steve called on day six to tell me two things. First, he did not want to work in a shop, write about motorcycles or sell them. I said great, you learned a lot because it's critical in a career search to know what you don't want to do before you blindly send resumes for jobs you'll find you dislike doing. He agreed and admitted he had sent two resumes to sales jobs. Now that he knew how much time it took, how sales compensation worked and the travel demands, he knew he would not be happy in sales.

The second thing he told me was supposed to surprise me – but I already knew how the secret worked. You see, listening and talking to people about what they are interested in, what's going on in their lives often provides you information you need to help them and occasionally it helps you. Steve had found out that the repair shop owners wife worked for a large insurance company as a Project Manager.

Steve didn't really know what a Project Manager did in a large company so he asked if he could talk to her and find out more about the company and project management. The shop owner was more than happy to help. Steve had given him a hint on how to do something easier while repairing a bike and the owner wanted to return the favor.

Steve could barely contain his excitement. He told me that he already had the call with her. She knew enough about him from her husband's conversation that she invited another manager and an HR representative to the call. By the end of the call, they scheduled time for Steve to visit and at the end of that visit he was hired. The job was never posted. He never submitted a resume. The company had three more project manager positions open. Two were filled by internal candidates and one by a referral Steve made. Steve was already sharing the secret and helping others.

Steve has been working there for seven years. You see, that's the way it works. That's the "secret". Transitioning out of the service is one of the most challenging things you will ever do and most of us will be unsuccessful at first. In fact, 65%+ of all Veterans leave the first job they take after active duty (Military Times).

I believe the root causes are the ineffective career search advice, lack of networking skills, and absence of a fellow veteran who has "been there, done that, got the t-shirt" to help coach, introduce, and support you. And one who knows the secret! I was so proud to have helped another Veteran find the job he wanted, and it all started with the first job I had after leaving the Army.

At my first job with the WA State DVA, there was a retired MSgt. who worked tirelessly to help veterans receive VA benefits – especially homeless Vietnam combat veterans. We were talking one day, and I asked him why he put so much of himself and so many hours into his work. I remember his response to this day, "Stu, once you've served, you can never stop serving. With or without the uniform, our job is to help those to the left and right of us. That's why we fight so hard and so well, because of those next to us". I never served in combat, but I serve my fellow veterans "in the fight" by making their transition a little easier.

Find your passion. Help your fellow Veterans. Keep serving and share the secret. "Hooah and "Always First" 3/1 Infantry, Queen of Battle"!

LL #21: Behavioural is where it's at!

Eric "Doc" Wright, USN & USARNG

Along with "Do not speak military", you'll also hear "Make sure to prepare for your interviews!". How? Here is one way to help you prepare:

1. Find companies on LinkedIn you would like to work with based on: (1) their social media image, (2) values, (3) industry, (4) work descriptions, and (5) reputation.

2. Then, connect with people on LinkedIn that work inside those companies. Ask them how the company treats its employees, each other, and customers. Ask them how they do projects and what type of management styles reign. Ask them about their bosses. Ask them about their hiring and promotion interviews. Ask them about problems their company and industry face. Ask them what credentials are valued. Ask them how they dress.

This is all great intelligence for your interview questions for them, and for your answers to theirs! Your questions will be meaningful and demonstrate preparation and insight, and your answers will be familiar to them, their company, and their challenges and opportunities. You will be familiar; interested in them and their company. And it will be conversational, which helps them see you as a team member!

LL #22: You must bring a belt, sock, shoe game?

Eric "Doc" Wright, USN & USARNG

We have spent years wearing the same uniforms, which changed only depending on the situation or season. And someone told us what that uniform of the day was!

Not so in the CIVDIV.

However, there are nuances to their 'uniforms', i.e. business dress, too. Things like:

• Men: for an interview, which you always overdress for, wear a pocket square, match your shoe and belt color, wear traditional, *fitted* suits, like Navy, Black, or Charcoal Gray, with ties. Add color laces if you want to be flashy, but a sock game and pocket square should do it.

• Women: for an interview, wear slacks or a skirt, a nice blouse, jacket, or cardigan sweater; or a dress. Don't wear sandals or shoes that are too high. Always overdress for an interview. If they say business casual for an interview you should still wear a pants suit, skirt and jacket, or nice dress.

- All: go easy on the perfume and cologne, jewelry, and make-up. You want to be memorable for your well prepared and articulately delivered meaningful behavioral answers. Your look should augment, not detract.

LL #23: Mediocrity, comparatively, is the new standard!

Jeremy Burdick, USAF

All of us, veterans included, have worked with dirtbags that should have been separated two assignments ago but instead they are squirreled away in some position and left to their own misguided ways, only to find out they were promoted again.

In the civilian world, it seems the population of dirtbags went up per captia (or population) by at least three times! What was a thorn is now a rose? Why, you ask?

In the service, you had ten people in the unit and one or two were dirtbags, which meant you now needed eight people to do the work of ten and there was no getting rid of the dead weight. There was certainly no failing. Thus, your team always tried to exceed the standard because the standard was a just a measuring stick for the others not you.

In the civilian world showing up on-time, being drug-free, and going through the motions at your job is the standard. Here the standard is acceptable. You are used to taking the standard and exceeding it, that means you will stand out like a wolf amongst sheep. Sounds scary for the sheep, it is, so let's minimize it.

Maybe throw a sheep sweater over your wolf exterior. You will still be a wolf under it but now you are camouflaged. Make your bosses look great! If you have a good idea, do not throw it out in public and gloat, run it by your immediate supervisor and let them take credit for it. Sounds ridiculous to just give away your idea, well not really, they will take care of you when it is time, besides this is what you do, and it is not some epiphany it is your normal.

You will become invaluable to them; moreover, you are the new guy and "new guys" cannot have good ideas (insert giggle here, remember sheep sweater). Keep the sweater theory going in most aspects, be the hero you are just turn the volume down a bit, we do not want to spook the herd. Lastly, never compromise your values or your ability to lead later. What I mean is, your actions and behavior will echo far longer than you think.

LL #24: Learn to brag! Fast!

Eric "Doc" Wright, USN & USARNG

In the service, it was about others, the team, and the branch first. Selfless service, right? It's typically opposite in the CIVDIV; it is about me, me, and did I mention? Me.

To set your expectation, a Monster.com survey found that many in the CIVDIV not only brag about their accomplishments, but that they sometimes exaggerate, lie, omit information, or take credit for things they did not do.[14] No doubt the immense focus and pressure the CIVDIV places on individual performance contributes.

However, do not let your integrity and humility take you out of the hiring or promotion running! Sure, talk about what your team accomplished, for the organization, just make sure to highlight *your* active role in producing the results or the environment that facilitated the success.

---

[14]   https://www.monster.com/career-advice/article/the-truth-about-resume-lies-hot-jobs

It will probably always remain a bit uncomfortable for you to some degree; it still is for me even after 20+ years of doing it. But you are your biggest advocate, so that others, your mentors, and managers, see your value, and become advocates for you!

LL #25: Networking is not just for jobs!

Eric "Doc" Wright, USN & USARNG

Not only do you need professional peers, but you also need professionals to keep you cavity free (dentist), nag you about your weight and BMI (personal trainer), tailor your suits (tailor), cut your hair (barber or stylist), and keep you square with the IRS (accountant). Your dentists, doctors, attorneys, accountants, barbers and stylists, and tailors are not just across the base from you anymore though, or on the main deck of the ship. They are scattered throughout your town, so you should spend some time finding them before you need them. Because you will.

LL #26: Get a barber or stylist!

Eric "Doc" Wright, USN & USARNG

I know you can cut your own hair, or always wear it pulled back. In fact, you have done it for years! But just because you can does not mean you should. Grow it out a bit. Add a bit of style. We can see you coming for miles away Regulation!

LL #27: No knife hands!

Eric "Doc" Wright, USN & USARNG

Use a single finger or pen to point to something. Additionally, Don't stand with your feet always shoulder width apart, toes pointed out at forty-five degree angles, with shoulders back. These things can frighten civilians! They sense your bearing is very different; it feels to them like you are not one of them.

LL #28: If it doesn't exist, create it.

Michael Klingshirn, USAF

I answered a random LinkedIn request in December and talked to a recruiter at Fusion Cell. We parted ways never expecting to hear from each other. Then COVID hit hard. We reconnected in March. This staffing agency made a pivot to consulting for COVID-19 recovery. I was their first choice for a COVID-19 consultant because of the conversation I had with the recruiter, my board certification in public health, and my PMP credentials.

There was a problem to be solved, a need across multiple industries, and people willing to invest time and money for the answer. We created a product that was used at multiple schools, offices, and even got into airports. I had calls with CEOs of fortune 500 companies and managers of 12-person operations at country clubs.

We built the aircraft as we were flying it, and everything we recommended was later validated when the CDC put out their guidance for those specific industries. Our product was far superior as it dug into the specifics of "how to", not just "consider the following". Fast forward to July. I was talking with the COO (now a daily call) and was offered a position with the company outside of the 1099 consulting agreements. I got an hour on the phone with a gentleman that sold a few companies for $100M+ over the years. This is something I would have never thought I would experience. Most importantly, I have helped schools in the US and the Bahamas create re-entry plans that safeguarded the health and safety of everyone within their walls.

All of this is possible for two reasons. First, I continue to seek recertification in the public health world. Second, my PMP certification made me the standout choice for starting, running, and now managing all consulting services.

Take those random calls. You never know what it will lead to in the future. If a potential customer has a need and you are reasonably sure you can hit the mark, promise them the world AND DELIVER! It takes long hours, but there is a lot to be said for making the CDC's plan before the CDC made their plan. This is applicable everywhere, not just for COVID. Get and maintain certifications. I have never used the board certifications I held to this extent while AD.

However, they gave me more credibility when making promises.

It is a scary job market. People have lost their livelihoods. It is an ideal time to take a chance and jump. Find a niche, create the standard, run the projects, and crush the expectations.

LL #29: Creating structure.

Eric "Doc" Wright, USN & USARNG

In the CIVDIV, there are no ranks, tabs, ribbons, unit crests, or other identifiable markings on their uniforms of the day, i.e. suits. So, to familiarize yourself to the CIVDIV quickly, ask for organizational charts. Recon your peers and managers on LinkedIn. Learn to identify them, but subtly. If you know you are sitting next to the COO, and you act like it and capitalize on it, you may get a head-start on the oblivious peers around you. Continue to carry that situational awareness you've honed so you can use it to your advantage.

LL #30: Focus on the front site!

Jeremy Burdick, USAF

Who are you? What do you want to do? Where do you want to live? And what does your family need when you leave the service? These are questions you need to answer. Don't just assume everything will be OK. There is lots of ambiguity, and little to no guidance. You have to paint a new end-state.

David Hume once stated, "there is no such thing as freedom of choice unless there is freedom to refuse". For the first time since you raised your hand at MEPS, you have the choice and the freedom to refuse "orders" without being liable under the UCMJ. There is a sense of gravity even as I type this and I have been retired for, at this point, 3 years.

I always had a sense of comfort in relegating my own choices for the greater good. Maybe it was the fact that I was not responsible for the choice? I did not come up with the policy, I just enforced it.

I see now how my attitude was a bit of a cop-out, but it did not really matter because my position was one of translating commander intent. When you transition it is time to ABOUT-FACE! You have focused on your nation's needs, now what are your needs, your family's needs, your potential employer's needs?

There will not be a guide, checklist, or standard procedure to be a grounding rod. You are building the process as you go.

First, remember you get the choice to refuse; however, you still need to be a hunter-gatherer (feed yourself, family, and employer), how much income do you need to be comfortable? Second, take some time and figure out what you want to do, what is enjoyable, what feels rewarding, or what are you skillful at? There is a business axiom that goes like this, "you bring something unique (skill, technique, experience) or you do it cheap (salary, schedule, location), everyone else is fighting for the middle. Third, get after it like it was a mission tasking. Do not passively check job boards, get Spec Ops on this, reverse engineer positions and match your resume for every position you submit for. Use a cover letter, get a business card, and send follow-up thank you letters. Talk to some free placement specialists like Cathy Miclat of Vets2PM (cathy@vets2pm.com) for placement on a free veteran talent bench called PurpleX. Finally, correct your vector based on feedback of people you trust or employers in industries you want to work in.

LL #31: Government Contracting Revenue Isn't Like Rain!

Eric "Doc" Wright, USN & USARNG

If you decide to start a business, which many veterans do, I encourage you to apply for and receive your Department of Veterans Affairs ("VA") veteran-owned small business ("VOSB")/service disabled veteran-owned small business ("SDVOSB") certification.[15] However, when you do, realize the work doesn't stop there. Contracts will not passively rain down on you like manna from heaven!

You'll have to chase the opportunities! Register in SAM.gov and beta.sam.gov. Determine your industry codes, called NAICS codes (North American Industry Classification Codes).[16] Form relationships with your area Procurement Technical Assistance Center.[17] This will help you learn about future opportunities you can bid on.

---

[15] https://www.va.gov/osdbu/verification/

[16] https://www.naics.com/search/

[17] https://www.aptac-us.org/

Pick up a copy of Joshua Frank's *An Insider's Guide to Winning Government Contracts* and Michael LeJeune's *Game Changers for Government Contractors*, and subscribe to RSM Federal's Federal Access digital toolbox.[18] These resources are chocked full of the templates, tools, tips, tricks, and processes you'll need to successfully generate a revenue stream from government contracting ("GOVCON"). Additionally, I am available to coach VOBs/SDVOSBs if you'd like.[19]

---

[18] www.federal-access.com

[19] https://rsmfederal.com/government-consulting-services

LL #31: Different promotion structure.

Eric "Doc" Wright, USN & USARNG

Promotions in the CIVDIV rely on hustle, merit, contributions to the manager and organization, profitability, and self-promotion, not longevity! Find mentors in positions you would like to have. Dress for the role you want, not the one you sit on now. Network inside your company to identify paths you would like to walk. Seek out professional development opportunities, which you can pursue on your own. Also look for training development opportunities that a company may provide, such as educational stipends or scholarships. All of these lead to being in a better position to get promoted while not stepping on others to get to the top.

LL #32: Missing the adrenaline rush.

Eric "Doc" Wright, USN & USARNG

The stress, pressure, and adrenaline rush you have felt during your time in uniform is likely not going to be the same when you are in your civilian job. Of course, there will be pressure and stress, but likely the job will not have life and death consequences. You just have to remind yourself that while you can thrive under intense mission-critical pressure, you do not have to anymore; just find challenges for yourself. Create your own pressure.

LL #33: Bring your resume A-game!

Cathy Miclat

Format, forward looking, "tailored", professional email address, cover letter as a story! That story should include what you want to do moving forward, supported by your experience and expertise acquired from your past.

Clean format: no pictures / photos, no graphics, no shadows, and absolutely no information in the header or in tables because the ATS cannot read that information! Headers and footers are for name and page number only. If you have a list of 'Areas of Expertise' or technical information that you want to put in a table...do not! Use the tabs or column functions. Do your best to keep it to two pages unless it is a Federal resume or a CV.

Resumes should be formatted in this manner:
- Top of page one: Name, city/state/zip, certifications, phone, LinkedIn link, email address
- Next; Header stating who/what you are. Example: Project Management | Program Management

- Next; Areas of Expertise; a 3 x 3 or 3 x 4 listing of key areas of expertise (project management, program management, logistics management, information technology, stakeholder engagement, process improvement, etc.)

- Next; Reverse chronological list of positions starting with current / most recent and moving backward. You do not need to detail career history more than 10 – 12 years or so; but it is a good idea to account for that time in a line such as this: Positions of Increasing Responsibility – Various Locations Year – Year

- Next; Education & Certification section. Here you can also list memberships, coursework, etc.

Keep it simple, clean, easy to read and #2 and #3 will ensure the reader can easily identify what you are all about during a quick few-second scan, so they will be enticed to read further!

Cover letter should support your match for a specific position; express your interest in the position, tell them why you fit that role, and ask for an interview. It should NOT reiterate your life or your entire resume.

Your resume and cover letter combine to tell your story, who you are, what you can do, and how that brings the company value. In first person.

LL #34: Tell your story!

Cathy Miclat

I recently posted on LinkedIn a meme of a lady sitting in front of a panel of 10 men who all look alike – it is called a 'panel interview,' and the question from the men was "Describe what you can bring to this company." To date, this post has 10,597 views and 78 comments. The comments are incredibly valuable to a Veteran preparing for their transition.

Highlights include:

- "Diversity"

- "Their job is to find the best person to do the work they need done, and to fit on the team. Your job is to be thoroughly prepared to convince them you are it! Start early and seek mentors who are experienced in the world you seek to join".

- "Once I'm onboard and get to know everyone here, I'll be able to replace at least three of them and do their work myself, in other words, 'Cost Savings.'"

- "The fact that I had sat for several award boards in the military helped tremendously, the struggle was translating my military experience into 'civilianese'. I was not prepared for that".

- "In order to be on par with your civilian counterparts / competition, you need to start your transition early. Why? Because your competition has been networking and establishing their corporate competencies while we were progressing with our military careers. Determine your professional identity in civilian terms; start networking based on that; and create a training plan for the remainder of your service time".

- "No matter how bad I think an interview goes, I most likely will not suffer a permanent injury and will most likely grow from whatever experience it had".

- "The purpose of this question, from a candidate's eyes, is to provide your future employer the reasons why they should hire you. Any candidate or person in sales lives for this question and should be able to provide five reasons why they are better".

- "If you know your stuff, you got it! Doesn't matter how many are there if you show up to win!"

- "Do not be afraid to toot your own horn and be your own greatest cheerleader. No one knows your accomplishments better than you. Keep it short and sweet (KISS) to the job you are applying for and you will be just fine".

LL #35: The relationship of leadership and management.

Eric "Doc" Wright, USN & USARNG

Managers in the CIVDIV plan what they are going to do, including creating the performance standards and targets, resourcing their plan, leading the human resources in the execution of said plan, and controlling performance to ensure they deliver on the plan. With fiduciary responsibility, i.e. a responsibility to steward resources and produce profitability through increased revenue, decreased expenses, or both.

This doctrine is called Fayolism, or the general theory of business administration. It was created by Henri Fayol, a French mining engineer and executive, in 1903'ish. It has stood the tests of time, industry, company size, and it is the framework and doctrine every organization uses.

Even though we call ourselves leaders, in the CIVDIV, we are managers first, who lead as the third of four functions. The other three functions of a general manager in the CIVDIV are 1. Planning, 2. Organizing, and 4. Controlling. When we are good at leading, we rock! That is because most civilians do not have the amounts of formal and OJT leadership training we have had! Talk about your military leadership experience in this context, you demonstrate the full breadth and depth of your experience! You win in interviews and promotions!

LL #36: Is there really "stable employment"?

Eric "Doc" Wright, USN & USARNG

We wax nostalgic about the "good old days", when you could retire from a company that would take care of you, or a government that would provide you with a great pension. Have you read about what Congress is doing lately with regards to pensions? Yeah, they are making them private! And companies? My dad's company let him go at about fifty-five so they could defray retirement benefits, and he never found professional career success to that degree again. It was the late 80's, he was one of the first of countless casualties in the West's emerging corporate no loyalty campaign.

That is not stability! And it is not less risky!

MISSION TIP:
- Stay mobile.
- Stay hungry.
- Develop a free agent mentality! You might even consider starting a company. It may be far less risky to depend on yourself and your chops than put your eggs in some corporation's basket.

LL #37: Loss of mission, purpose, and identity.

Eric "Doc" Wright, USN & USARNG

One of the most pressing but least talked about challenges of the military transition is the immediate, and very profound, loss of mission, identity, and purpose.

It happened to me and I could not even articulate what was plaguing me!   And it almost killed me!

Career fields like project management, human resources, cyber security, building safety, big data, and the like can help. Look for work where what you do is meaningful, where you are the responsible, accountable expert in delivering the goods and services, and success means the organization flourishes. It can help you maintain a sense of mission, purpose, and identity. And get a wee bit of adrenaline through challenges here and there!

MISSION TIPS:

- Check out:
  - Project Management Institute at www.pmi.org
  - Cyber Bytes Foundation at https://cyberbytesfoundation.org/
  - Applied Technology Academy at https://appliedtechnologyacademy.com/
  - Correlation One at https://www.correlation-one.com/
  - International Code Council at https://www.iccsafe.org/professional-development/safety2/
  - Hildebrand Solutions at https://www.hildebrandsolutions.com/
  - AgileDad at https://www.agiledad.com/
  - Vets2PM at www.vets2pm.com

LL #38: Receive and pay it forward.

Craig A. Jones, USMC

Seek out a mentor. Or mentors for that matter. There are many formal and informal ways to do this. There are formal programs that will pair you with mentors based on your stated wants and needs. Some examples are the Veteran Project Manager Mentor Alliance, Veterati, Veteran Mentor Network, and American Corporate Partners.

There are also plenty of opportunities to informally seek out folks to gain advice from. Being a mentee is great. We all can learn from others that may have already made the mistakes we can now skip or have opportunities for us to grow and develop.

There is no formula on who to seek out or when to seek them out. Do it now and seek out many folks. Some will be of short-term benefit. Others may be of longer-term benefit. That is okay! Use everyone as a small piece to your own puzzle. Own it and put it together as you go.

Also, be a mentor. Mentees need what you have to offer, and they need it now! You will find that by also being a mentor you will learn, thus growing and developing just as much as being a mentee. Together we can!

LL #39: Military achievements need translated!

Jeremy Burdick, USAF

I was told my military achievements will carry and translate to the civilian companies and hiring managers. The truth is the above statement could not be more misleading; you must become the translator. Civilian managers do not understand that while you were enduring hostile fire, you resupplied a Navy Seal and Seabee contingent at an African French Foreign Legion Field not intended to have aircraft of any substantial size land but most importantly take back off. While coordinating with operations and maintenance from 6,000 miles away at a daytime-only field with the sun going down, we coordinated a major mechanical waiver through multiple leadership echelons to recover a $30 million dollar asset. In the eyes of the hiring manager, they say "and, how does that translate into you bringing in revenue, turning gross revenue into net revenue, or retaining earnings?"

Well boss, with minimal communication or technology support, our project team utilized the communication plan to address various stakeholders' risk appetite. We then implemented our risk plans to address the loss of $30 million dollars in assets compared to the loss of human life. Next, we utilized multi-criteria decision through SMEs to ensure both customer procurement fulfillment on-time and asset reallocation to the home organization by activating a work-around procedure. This resulted in organization-wide recognition, an airframe first-ever event, returning seven employees to daily operations, and generating a new-supply channel. How does that sound boss?

LL #40: Understand your value.

Cathy Miclat

A transitioning Air Force Officer was willing to interview for a basic entry level position in a local healthcare system because her mentors told her she would 'have to start her civilian career from the ground floor.' Not true. After discussing her responsibilities in uniform, I was able to present them to her in 'civilian' language and examples which enabled her to see her value to industry and boost her confidence in her skills and expertise. She approached her job search from this new perspective, and Booz Allen Hamilton created a position for her, earning six figures (plus). She earned a leadership position because her 24+ years in uniform prepared her for a role in a Fortune 500 organization, and she gained the confidence to go for it with authority!

LL #41: Understand your goals.

Cathy Miclat

A U.S. Army Aviation / Aircraft Maintenance Veteran transitioned in 2014, took four years to go to college post transition, earning a BS in Professional Aeronautics; MS in Leadership; and MBA in Aviation, and ended up in a job managing a family contracting (construction) business. His education and Army experience weren't enough to get him to his dream job at Boeing...so he registered for PMP training and received help translating his experience on his resume into a) terms that the CIVDIV could understand, and b) targeting a specific company. He called me in tears immediately after accepting the job with Boeing, and two weeks before his relocation to WA state to thank me for the help.

MISSION TIP:

• Understand your goals, work hard to achieve them, and ask for help. If he had not asked for help, he would likely still be working for that family contracting business. Sometimes you do not know what you do not know, and while you are doing everything right, you need that extra bit of assistance to get you to the peak!

LL #42: Sometimes you are a threat!

Jeremy Burdick, USAF

You threaten people! Okay, what I mean is, you carry yourself like you defended freedom (check), led people into harm's way (check), and translated strategic vision into tactical actions (check). So, what is the hiring manager supposed to think? The idea is not to dumb down your demeanor or filter who you are or what you did but rather to elevate the company you are trying to get into. Present a value proposition or a scenario where the hiring manager is the hero for finding such amazing talent.

During your interview, do not talk about money or salary (unless they bring it up) then just like hostile negotiations deny, deflect, and defeat. Interviewer asks, "how much money would you like to make?" Your response, "that is a great question, I have been so busy making sure I am the best (insert interviewing job title), I figured the recruiters here would be better at assessing my value based on the assigned responsibilities, workload, and geographical compensation averages." So, you just avoided a pitfall question, denied the enemy (not really the enemy) critical information, deflected the question back to your skills, then defeated the engagement. Also, you just made them feel better as you have acknowledged their expertise in the market.

The truth is they are experts in the field, the area, and the organization. They have the essential elements of information you require to make an intelligent response. You do not walk up to surgeon and say, "give me the scalpel, I can take out my own appendix". No, you let them do their job, and the recruiter's job is to assess your talent, skills, and fit for the company.

LL #43: Get liquid...FAST!

Steven B. Crane, USMC

Many people are going to tell you to save a lot of money and pay off debt, and while this is all great advice, sometimes, it is just not possible. If you find yourself in this situation, try to become as liquid as possible. Cash is king, and it will undoubtedly create a safety net for you as you prepare to transition from the military. If this means selling some electronics, furniture, collectibles, then do it. The more money you have on hand now, the easier it will be to weather the storm. If you are interested in learning about managing your money during this tough time, please visit https://www.daveramsey.com/ for common sense money tips that have helped millions of people become financially independent.

LL #44: File for Unemployment.

Steven B. Crane, USMC

While every state has its own unique benefits, they offer to their military veterans, be sure to check with your state to see if you qualify for unemployment. For example, an honorably discharged E-5 in Ohio qualifies for about $350/week. Although $350/week is nothing to get excited about, it certainly can help during the adjustment period as you get settled in with the VA. Every state has its own requirements, so be sure to research it and apply it as soon as you separate from the military. If you are interested in learning more about unemployment and see if you qualify, please visit https://www.usa.gov/unemployment for more information about how you can receive up to 50% of your paycheck after you separate from the military.

LL #45: Take a 30-day vacation.

Steven B. Crane, USMC

Transitioning from the military is one of the most stressful periods of your life. While I am not excusing you from your responsibility to face the world and do what you have to do to survive, I would recommend taking a month off to get your affairs in order. Go research some schools, get your medical paperwork taken care of with the VA, see what benefits your state offers to military veterans, etc. During these 30 days, try your best to forget about the military and begin to view yourself as a successful civilian, not just a military veteran. After you have taken 30 days to get your house in order, then I would turn my focus on a career, or enrolling in a school. The important thing is that you take a little time to acclimate yourself back into a civilian regiment by focusing on taking care of you for a change, and not everyone around you.

LL #46: Never accept the first thing the VA tells you.

Steven B. Crane, USMC

If you are like most veterans, you were injured or sustained some sort of medical issue throughout your military career. Additionally, you probably have filed for your VA disability rating, and you may have already received an answer. Now again, if you are like most veterans, you were somewhat disappointed in the answer you initially received. Perhaps you were rated at 40% when you know deep down that you should easily be at 90% or 100%. As someone who has been through this gauntlet, and has helped many others go through this battle, I can almost assure you that you were underrated.

Now the reasons may differ from person to person, but more than likely, you were evaluated by a VA doctor or someone who is contracted by the VA to conduct your evaluation. Most veterans just need a helping hand through this process by working with organizations such as https://www.REEMedical.com.

If you have not already begun this fight, I urge you to contact them and see if they are able to assist you. Veterans take care of our own, and there is no better feeling than receiving the rating you deserve. Do yourself a favor and begin this process as soon as possible...your family, health, and future self will thank you!

LL #47: Always treat yourself like a company.

Steven B. Crane, USMC

When you are transitioning from the service, you will hear people tell you to build a brand and to know what you want to do. While this is great advice, …where does one begin? When companies are formed, a vision, strategy, mission, and values are established, and it helps guide the company to success. I advise people to do the same with themselves early in their careers and continue to shape it through the years. The first thing to think about is, what values do you currently live by? Do not think about what you "want" to live by, but instead, how do you currently live your life? Next, envision the future and think about a perfect vision of what the 40 – 50 – 60-year-old self of you looks like? During this stage, it is perfectly normal to have a very vague idea of what it looks like. For example, you could envision yourself working at a company as a Senior VP, or maybe you are traveling the world with your family. Whatever your vision is, capture it in writing.

Next is to develop your mission, which could be as simple as what are a few things you wish to accomplish within the next year that will help get you closer to the vision. For example, if you envisioned being a Professor at a university, have you enrolled in college? Have you spoken with a professor? Do you know what you want to get your bachelor's, master's, and a doctorate in? The key to remember is that your action items may change from year to year; however, so long as you are continuously taking steps towards your vision, and living by your values, you are just one step closer to achieving your dream. Above all else, practice being authentic and let that drive your story. If you are interested in learning more about authentic leadership and how to create your path, please check out Discover Your True North & Authentic Leadership by Bill George and be sure to purchase the workbook for clear directions on how you can leverage your past failures to help you achieve success.

LL #48: Unconventional jobs lead to conventional skills for success.

Steven B. Crane, USMC

Story Time! – When I was transitioning from the military, I experienced what so many veterans, unfortunately, go through…underemployment. However, while some people may view it simply as a way to put food on the table, I viewed each position as an opportunity to explore new skill sets and add to my arsenal of tools and techniques that will assist me later in life. As I explain my journey from Marine Corps veteran to where I am now, I encourage you to reflect back on your personal experience and try to see how the unconventional jobs you may have had can translate into conventional skills for your success.

As I was exiting the military, I chose to become a financial advisor because I wanted to help people manage their finances and become financially independent. However, as I learned more about the industry, the regulations, and potential long-term opportunities, the job I once wanted was no longer attractive. While I began to transition into a different job, I collected all of my thoughts on my experience and began to realize that I learned some very valuable lessons.

Among many things, I learned the importance of continuous education as a civilian, hustling to get what you want, relationship management, sales, marketing, presenting in front of a class, emotional selling tactics, regulatory compliance, and financial knowledge. While many would stop there and take the obvious lessons learned and translate it into their next job, I went one step further and thought about every ounce of information I took away. Things such as how to dress for different occasions, how to physically position yourself in a conversation, how to shake hands with different people, how to have a business meeting with a client over coffee, and even how to read and mirror body language. While these skills may not directly transfer into a great career, they are invaluable skills of senior leaders and executives that some people never truly master.

My next major job was as a car salesman for Toyota. Yes, I was the stereotypical new/used car salesman that sold anything I could get my hands on. Although the thrill of the hunt was exhilarating and the feeling of closing a deal was a high, I ultimately learned that it was not something I could see myself doing when I was 50 years old. So, I followed the process that I previously did and collected all of the tangible and intangible lessons from this position. Again, I took a very different approach than most people would when assessing the duties and responsibilities of a car salesman.

Some of the key things I took away from this position were the ability to build a relationship and establish trust in under an hour, how to be competitive with coworkers without making enemies, how to correctly critique someone's presentation, the ability to laugh at my mistakes and roll with the punches, being comfortable in my skin in the way I present something to someone, and most importantly, the confidence to excite others about an idea or product that is being sold to them. While these attributes or skills are not going to be listed on a job application, they are essential in today's work environment and immediately distinguishes someone from the rest of the pack.

After leaving Toyota as a car salesman, my next position was very unconventional but proved to be one of the most valuable experiences. I became a case broker for a personal injury law firm in which I leveraged my sales experience to convince people that their misfortune could result in serious compensation. Once a person agreed to become a client, we would then sell the case to attorneys across the nation who would represent them in their case. This position completely changed the way I saw not only customers but sales in general.

I grew incredibly empathetic towards others, their personal situations, and developed a much bigger appreciation for those who work in call centers. The sheer volume of cases we handed on a daily basis was something I could have never fathomed. However, as with previous positions, all good things must come to an end and I decided to leave that position after acquiring some new skills that would assist me later down the road. My time at the law firm taught me the importance of understanding personalities, how to transfer information from a client to a senior executive, how to communicate and sell on the phone, the importance of respecting, connecting, and protecting people during times of turmoil, how to capture the attention of different audiences, and lastly, realizing that every company uses different software programs and learning how to master them quickly.

My experience at the law firm was one that I will never forget because of the emotional connection I built with people who were suffering and needed help. Again, while this is probably never going to help you meet the qualifications for a job, it was the opportunity to grow as a leader that thrilled me.

Following my natural curiosity with sales, I decided to go off and become a REALTOR® to expand my skillset. I became licensed and went straight to work in helping people through the home purchasing/selling process. The interesting thing about being a REALTOR® is that no one tells you what to do, and it is up to you to generate business and develop your client base. Again, my experience in being a REALTOR® taught me some valuable lessons such as developing a brand, selling yourself and not a service, the importance of asking the right questions – at the right time, the value of nurturing a relationship over time through follow-ups, the fact that people do not care what you know until they know how much you care, how to strategize as a small business and grow a company, and most importantly, it is not about what you know OR who you know, it is ALL about who knows you!

After being a REALTOR®, I realized there was one thing I had not sold…insurance. So, after some training and licensing, I became a life & health insurance salesperson. By this time, I had experience in financial coaching, automobiles, legal cases, and even homes, so I was eager to learn what new things I could learn from this position. I was quickly inundated with a whole new world of employee benefits, health insurance, life & death benefits, and much more. However, despite all of the new information, I was able to leverage previous experiences to assist me in my transition.

Some key takeaways from this job were the importance of story-telling, the value of humility in a very competitive space, how to quickly learn and pass certification exams, the ability to think quickly on my feet and facilitate workshops, what it truly means to be an entrepreneur and intrapreneur, how to see things from a different perspective and shift my message for better comprehension accordingly, finally, how to accept no for an answer and keep a positive attitude for the next customer. All of these are highly sought-after skills and traits; however, if you never take a step back and see the bigger picture, you can miss out on invaluable qualities you too can add to your toolbox.

Aside from these experiences, I also:

- Started my own company

- Cleaned residential and commercial properties

- Sold home cleaning systems

- Coached & mentored other veterans who transitioned from the military

- Helped start a non-profit

- Did undercover investigations – (this could be a whole book itself ha-ha!)

- Assisted others in starting their own businesses

- Managed contracts for a $400M company

- And to cap it off – I was a full-time student in college during all of this

I mentioned all of this to tell you one important thing – it does not matter where you start; it is all about growing from the journey to get you to where you are going. This may sound altruistic in nature, but if top people like Gary Vaynerchuk are preaching the importance of loving the grind and being patient, then call me crazy, but I agree! So long as you are giving 100% of your effort and living like today is the last day, you should enjoy the journey. Every position, whether you are a janitor (been there done that) or you are selling vacuums (did that too), or even managing contracts between major national fast-food chains (yup, that one too), will have their ups and downs.

The key is to look beyond the day-to-day responsibilities and find ways to better yourself and improve on basic skill sets. Something I always tell people is, "Do what you can, when you can, so when you can't, it's not a big deal".

What I want you to take away from all of this is to keep an open mind with everything you do and be mindful of how the daily duties you perform could eventually land you a killer career. You never know when the small skills and traits you develop today may come in handy later in life!

LL #49: Fail fast!

Raphael Montgomery, US Army ("USA")

In the military, most of us were fortunate to be surrounded by and to be a part of great Teams. Failure was not an option. Transitioning is a whole new story. While there are more and more organizations and networks to help you navigate the process, none can prepare you for "no." In the last 4 months of my service, I submitted for 33 different jobs in my area. Some of these companies I never heard back from, which is a common practice in the civilian sector, they do not move with the same urgency we do in the military. Others responded back within 4-6 weeks, all with a "thank you for applying, but we will continue with applicants that more closely align with what we are looking for". That is tough to hear / read and tough on the ego.

Once I was told "no" a few times, I realized it is not personal, there are other candidates out there every bit as good and possess industry experience, making them more qualified. You can overcome this by leveraging your network and ensuring your resume is tailored to the job description. "Fail Fast" is an agile principle that stresses it is okay to fail early in a process. The key is, how can you take that failure and learn from it? It is also good to get "no" out of the way and understand how this new environment works.

LL #50: Leave your ego at the door and have a slice of humble pie...

Patrick Pressoir, Canadian Forces

When I transitioned from a 14-year military career to the private sector, I did not have much relevant experience on my resume. It was basically a summary of all my postings and what I did there. I was still young, but I was eager to transition (and I certainly did not have access to all the resources available now) so I ended up settling for a job significantly below my pay grade. I figured I would have to basically start over.

As a result, I was frustrated, and in a sense resentful, for many years that my military experience was not recognized as pertinent. It got to the point that my resume was like a conveyor belt; as I gained new CivDiv experiences, I would drop off the older military ones. I had my sights set on the time where eventually, I would not even have any military experience on there at all. That way I could avoid any potential discrimination.

The problem is these were just stories I was telling myself. It was my ego talking and I was the one discriminating against my military experience because I just could not see how to properly articulate the parallels in CivDiv terms. I was so set in the regimented Army speak that I just could not (and would not) make the translation. "If they don't see that leading a unit of 50 soldiers includes ensuring their welfare, their development, managing their performance and operating budgets, collectively achieving objectives, setting and monitoring key indicators, do I really have to spell all that out for them?"

I know my stubbornness to translate my experience cost me many opportunities for advancement and repelled many recruiters because of the language and experience I chose to put on my resume.

At the end of the day, you have to realize that our experience IS RELEVANT, it is just that we do not speak the same language as the CivDiv, and we have to keep our ego in check. We cannot expect recruiters to understand what goes into planning an exercise or developing and executing an annual training plan – we must articulate those things in business terms.

When you think of it, we are managers, human resources, organizational development, project managers, strategic planners, and on and on. It is just a question of finding the parallels and bringing them to light.

So, do yourself a favor and do not make the same mistake I did. It sabotages your career and really misrepresents what you are truly capable of. Just leave your ego at the door and have a slice of Humble Pie....The sooner you come to realize that all our military training and lingo means nothing in CivDiv (on the surface) the better you will position yourself for the transition. Take the time to learn the CivDiv lingo and to find the parallels to your own experience – then adjust your resume accordingly. They are not discriminatory toward service people – they just need to understand how what we did is relevant.

LL #51: Brilliance in the basics.

Mark Hannah, USMC

Marines fight with agility and operate with structure and a right-time ability to adjust. This ability to "adapt" by pivoting through innovative risk averse thinking requires both military leadership principles and traits (courage). From executives to line managers what I learned as the Basics of teamwork and leadership is a Herculean change management challenge because the warrior culture does not align with civilian culture.

LL #52: MILSpeak vs CIVDIV.

James McCulley, USA

Transitioning from the military and all the acronyms, nomenclature, and military jargon to what Dr. Wright calls the "CIVDIV" was so much easier after going through the Vets2PM course. Once you realize that everything you did in the military relates back to one piece of the PM puzzle in some shape or fashion, it makes the transition so much smoother.

LL #53: More about MILSpeak vs CIVDIV.

Cathy Miclat

Before you begin interviewing for jobs in the CivDiv, read anything you can about business, and more specifically about your chosen industry. Listen to podcasts. Seek informational interviews. Use every opportunity you can to become comfortable with the new language you are going to be expected to know. Immerse yourself. Learn the lingo. Practice using the new vernacular.

The Institute of Certified Professional Managers curriculum and credential can help you do this and prove it. This will help when you begin landing interviews. Ask family and friends what military terms you use on a regular basis and find out what the civilian equivalent is, and practice using it. You do not want the 'knife hand' or unknown words slipping out during an interview!

LL #54: Always be learning.

Joey Eisenzimmer, USMC

Learning has become democratized thanks to many online resources. Some are free and some are paid, but it has never been easier to learn a new skill especially those that focus on technology. During your transition it is important to invest in yourself through training that focuses on your career of interest. For example, if you are going into Corporate America the PMP or ACP make great investments because you can leverage your military experience and instantly relate to employers.

I would also highly recommend devoting time to learn in-demand tech skills like SQL, software development and cloud principles, and potentially how to code. You do not have to be the foremost expert, but the more tools in your tool belt, the better prepared you'll be to hit the ground running in the CIV-DIV. Businesses and technology are moving faster than ever, and it's important to set yourself up for success. Always be learning!

LL #55: Break the habit of self-sacrifice.

Carlos V. Ulibarri, USA

Throughout our time serving, we are taught to sacrifice many of our personal desires in order to support our country's mission. In doing so, we have collectively accomplished great things as a military. Sacrifice becomes deeply ingrained in our psyche over time. And many of our personal ambitions have been an afterthought. Without guilt or judgment, consider investing your time and energy into your own goals.

If you don't think you have it in you to be self-centered for a while, consider what you might be able to contribute after you have built yourself into the person you want to be. It is extremely difficult to build yourself into that person if you are constantly giving pieces of yourself to others.

LL #56: It is never too early to start your transition!

James Onder, USAF

Being service members, we have great skills, training, and a lot of qualities that employers are looking for. Many people told me that "you'll have no problems finding a job with all your years of service". This is not great advice. While we do have a lot of things employers are looking for, we have gaps to fill as well.

My transition started at about 18 months out, setting goals to fill those gaps. I was in the Air Force Civil Engineering community and served 26 years. I knew my experience would be recognized, but to compliment it I obtained my bachelor's degree in Management, and my PMP in hopes to better round out my resume. I took advantage of any transition program I could find. Then I started to network, and sell myself anywhere I could...LinkedIn, local networking events, etc. I wanted to meet people in the field I was trying to work in, or those who knew people who did.

My experience, credentials, and network got me the job I wanted. Transitioning from military service can be very unsettling, and I was VERY nervous. I recently spoke to a Vets2PM Boot Camp class about my transition, and the one question I will never forget..."How early should I start my transition?" My answer was simple..."It's never too early".

LL #57: Your rank may not mean anything to civilians.

Misty Moreno, USAF

I have been on my military transition journey since Mar 2020. I have applied to 50 jobs, had 6 interviews, & received 1 solid offer. In my interviews, I answered questions about being female in the military, holding a high rank, and how I felt about "actually doing work".

There are companies out there that appreciate military service and want to help vets. But there are some that say they want to, but their actions say different. I have been told my entire career that companies will find me and want to hire me because of my experience and rank. But the truth is, my rank is just not important to most outside of the military.

I wanted to share because I know a lot of you are about to transition. Please reach out and pick my brain. I want to help you.

Lastly, if you have not started doing these 5 things, STOP WHAT YOU ARE DOING AND START NOW!!!!!

1. Make the military a part of your life versus your life.

2. Find your purpose and self-worth in other things besides the military.

3. Establish a community of people outside of the military.

4. Define what a "successful" or "smooth" transition looks like.

5. Decide your salary range...low, medium, high. My low salary pays the bills.

Standing by if you need help!

LL #58: I had to learn the hard way.

Paul DeJarnette, USAF

I had to learn the hard way that the way the military perceives risk, and approaches Project Management as a result is, very different than the civilian environment.

Be humble and remember that it is ok not to know everything; learn to accept risk as a positive player in project management.

LL #59: You're not in Kansas anymore.

Philip Hicks, USAF

What are your expectations after being in the military? The military puts skilled people in leadership positions under highly stressful (sometimes combat) situations. Most leaders of the companies and organizations you are entering have extensive experience in the company, market, and business. You can expect to probably not start out at the top of an organization. But you can successfully work your way to the top by employing the skills developed during your military career. Continue to use the skills that made your military career a success and develop new skills. Broaden your leadership skills beyond the autocratic directing method of the military because the civilian marketplace looks for consensus building for implementation of plans of action.

One definition of "persona" from Merriam Webster's Dictionary is "an individual's social facade or front that especially in the analytic psychology of C. G. Jung reflects the role in life the individual is playing." Your military persona as "Lieutenant Colonel," "Major," "Command Sergeant Major," "Chief Master Sergeant," etc. no longer exists. While respected by military outsiders, you are no longer that individual. You are a singular person providing skills and abilities to an organization. What value can you provide to the company? How are you improving the bottom line? The transition from an identified military member to a civilian can be the most trying. I hope and pray everyone has established a strong moral and ethical base for the transition because this will help you identify the person you want to be after you retire. I pray your faith, voluntary efforts, and family will help you define who you will be in the future.

Final notes...remember you are not alone in this journey. Remember to reach out to friends, family, and your support systems for help during your transition. The resources available to military members during transition are many, but they are useless if not accessed.[20]

---

[20] https://www.linkedin.com/pulse/20141024143510-168102092-my-military-retirement-journey/

LL #60: Breathe.

Clint Gershenson, USA

Transitioning from the military into the civilian world can be stressful. Jokes that were a coping mechanism for the darkness experienced in the military get awkward glances around the water cooler, people do not appreciate being yelled at, most decisions that are not life and death, and leading from the front is not necessary all the time.

I found the biggest tool for transitioning into the civilian world is something we all have...breath. You breathe about 23,040 times in a day. This tool can be instrumental in many areas from getting a job to leading and coaching teams. I have found breathing to be quite important in job interviews, reduction in stress, and avoiding awkward moments.

Job interviews can be quite tough. For most of your military career, you focus on rote knowledge. Memorizing everything you can from creeds to field manuals. While this can be important to get promoted in the military, the civilian world asks a plethora of experience and situational questions.

Aside from the fact that breathing will keep you from passing out during the interview, you can use something called the thoughtfulness breath. When you get asked a question, stop, take a breath, think, and answer. The intentional breath you take right after a question gives your brain the juice it needs to carefully connect your experience and knowledge to formulate a well-crafted response. This response is also delivered in a calmer state leading to the impression of confidence that companies look to hire.

Once you land that job of yours, you will soon realize that some civilian organizations do not run as smoothly as you remember your units/teams running in the military...even if you are just glorifying your memories of the military. This will cause stress, stress that is actually quite hard to manage if you do not take the time to breathe. Science has shown a reduction in stress when we stop and just breathe.

Stress is not the only thing we should avoid; we should also avoid a once acceptable vocabulary in the workplace. In the military, many folks swear like a sailor or use dark inappropriate humor around the clock. I have learned from experience that co-workers that have never had to be around dead people or the darkness of war DO NOT understand humor as a coping mechanism.

When you want to go down the swearing like sailor or dark humor road, I urge you to stop, take a breath, and ask yourself if what you are about to say is going to be helpful to them or to you attaining your goals. If the answer is no, do not say it. Eventually, your new habit or talking less like a sailor will guide you towards greater responsibility in the company.

Becoming a leader in the organization will soon follow once you show yourself as a calm, collected, and motivated person. As a leader in the organization, breathing becomes even more important. Use breath to instill confidence in your team. In the Military it is imperative to mission success that you have a high performing team. Creating high performing teams will not happen if we are always telling the team what to do. Provide the strategy up front and ensure everyone understands the why. Once you are confident the team understands the why, be quiet and breathe. In meetings, do not dominate, sit back, take a breath, and let the team figure out how to solve a problem, or how to answer a question. People naturally fill the silence with words.

Breathing is one of those natural things that we do not think much about. As you can see above, I have pointed out a few uses that can be beneficial for you and your careers. There are many techniques and all of them have some science backing them up. Search for them online and see what works for you. Remember to stop, breathe, and continue if you are adding value.

LL #61: Connect the dots.

Matthew Kolakowski, USA

With any transition in life, change comes frequently and unexpectedly. To this end, expect to transition from the military with these same frequent and unexpected bursts of change. While unexpected, the tides of transition and change can be navigated utilizing these three strategies to connect the dots:

Be open to opportunities given your documented skill sets. Once the military jargon is in a digestible format (Both for human and Applicant Tracking System eyes), start the process of investigating what you want to do with your experience. Sucking it up and "faking it until you make it" are not the ingredients of long-term professional and personal success. Before mapping your career, establishing a professional virtual presence, or obtaining civilian certifications, open yourself up to opportunity.

Know your role. Career upward mobility in the civilian sector is quite different from the military. To become a director, they do not send your performance records to a centralized board and then rank you. Instead, the intersection of willingness to learn, dependability, and demonstrated potential drive the process. Do not expect to be the CEO of an organization (Unless it is your own) immediately after exiting the military. Know your role and find something that you can excel in, and the promotions will come faster than you realize.

Professional Certifications are your Transition Friend. In the military, the enlisted and officer evaluation reports demonstrate to your command what you have done and are capable of doing. In the civilian sector, professional certifications (PMP, CPA, CFA, etc.) are your independent evaluation report. They show a willingness to demonstrate and reasonably prove that you possess a reasonably deep body of knowledge (BOK) in your profession.

While the transition process presents frequent and unexpected bursts of change, connecting the three dots above can serve as a starting point on your life's next journey.

LL #62: Do I need to keep my security clearance a secret?

Cathy Miclat

I am asked this question all the time, especially when speaking at career fairs for cleared professionals. Many people with high clearances do not believe they are allowed / should not share that information on a resume. I've researched this subject and have found that it is perfectly acceptable to state what your clearance level is...However, to state the obvious, you can't talk about what you do in your job that requires a clearance.

A security clearance can be a huge benefit to job searching – if you are going into government contracting or seeking a federal position, the clearance may be a requirement. It also does not hurt if you are going into private industry that is not government related. Most people are aware that many military service members have security clearances, and they know that there is a process to obtaining them, and it gives them confidence that you are an upstanding citizen in general, and will always do the right thing.

You can list your security clearance at the top of your resume and LinkedIn profile if you are seeking a career that requires it and can put it at the end of your resume if not.

LL #63: Common mistakes veterans make on the resume.

Cathy Miclat

A couple mistakes I see on a regular basis by transitioning military / Veterans who are writing their own resumes...

Placing contact information in the Header of the Word document is what I see most frequently. Please understand that many Applicant Tracking Systems (ATS) can't / do not read what is contained in the Header or Footer section of a Word document. Reserve that space for page numbers and your name, just so the document looks nice. Do not, and I repeat, do not put your name, email address, city, state, LinkedIn link, and phone number – or anything else you want to go into the ATS into the Header section of Word.

The second mistake I see most frequently is the use of 'tables' in Word. Much like the Header or Footer section, many ATSs cannot read what is contained in a table. People like to use the table section because they do not know how to use tabs. Google how to use tabs in Word, and you will get the hang of it. But...if you use a table you risk having all of that information eliminated from the ATS – which is what recruiters and talent acquisition professionals use to do key word searches to find you! Tables are often what people use to list key Areas of Expertise, Software, Systems, Technical expertise – these are all critical to finding a job, so do not use a table!

A way around this? Save your resume as a PDF. If the ATS accepts PDFs then you can use any feature in Word, and then save it as a PDF. I still believe Word is the best application to use for resumes, however, most ATSs accept PDF now and can support key word searching. Why do I still recommend using Word? Because there may be one ATS that does not accept PDFs, and then what will you do?

LL #64: Have a backup plan and be flexible.

"JB", USA

I had a very non-traditional career in the Army. The HR folks would send me to different assignments where I would have to learn a new system rapidly (Reserve Support, Theater Army Staff, Special Ops Support, Acquisition, BCT, etc.) I used this "agile" mindset when it came time to retire.

I was challenged with bringing my eclectic experiences to the "functional" logistics companies in the private sector. They were looking for SMEs on transportation, maintenance, warehouses. I ended up taking a high-risk security job as an operations manager. I had to convince the HR folks I could adapt to the company culture. I had a track record of "adapting".

Remember that separating veterans usually go through four to five jobs before they find a good "fit". Humility is key. The private sector HR folks do not really care about your overseas anecdotal accomplishments. You have to portray value to them. Or start your own business if you have the energy / capital.

I am working for a fourth company now. If the position does not work with my values / priorities, I start looking. We have worked too many years in sub-optimal units / positions to waste more time.

Be prepared to move where the jobs are. You are not a tree. Do not arrive at a new organization and start pointing out all the ways they are messed up. You may quickly find yourself marginalized, if not released. This happened to a guy I know (yuk, yuk). Lastly, take some time off. Work can be stressful, and you will be more effective if you are rested.

LL #65: Creative skill translations.

Robert Tyson, USA

I found that project specific translations of military skills to civilian employment is not difficult and should not be time consuming.

It is not as important to translate the hard skills because you [veterans] were doing what is expected of project managers by controlling scope, cost, and schedule already. It is the soft skill translations that will benefit you the most. It is the way you interact with stakeholders or translate their requirements that will get you the most traction, whether from an employer or how you learn from it...

LL #66: Military to Civilian Transition – Prepare for the future, not just the retirement.

Eric Paddock, USAF

We always hear the same advice "prepare for your retirement early". I never truly understood this advice until now. I mean, I was a 25-year Air Force Chief. I had a pension, and my skills were awesome (at least in my own mind), so what preparation did I truly need? Well, reality struck me pretty quickly after I removed my Service Dress and put on civilian clothes. I remember a conversation I had with another retiree around 3 months after I left the service and had been rejected from numerous jobs. He casually told me one day "Eric, in the Air Force you were someone….now, you're a no-one". Ouch!

That is when it finally hit home on what they meant by prepare for retirement. You see, in the Air Force, all I thought I needed to do was my TAPS and my VA processes. I did not really look past the retirement date; all of my energy was just focused on the event.

So, my advice is simple, look past the retirement and picture yourself doing something different. Then, start preparing for that vision. And do not start this preparation 6 month before you retire, start it years out. Change the way your write your performance reports to show that you are qualified in your future endeavor. Have a professionally written resume. (foot stomp!). We believe we know how to write in the military, but we do not. We speak a different language that our civilian counterparts do not understand. A professional resume writer will know how to translate our jargon into the correct language that a recruiter can read.

Finally, let the military go. No one cares what your previous rank was. Future recruiters care about experience, education, and certifications. If you lack education and certifications, get them before you retire. Transition Assistance and Air Force Cool are great tools to help you prepare for your future journey.
Final tidbit from a not so crusty old chief...enjoy the experience. There is a lot of anxiety and fear, but the freedom is so rewarding. Good luck and enjoy the journey.

LL #67: Break it down.

Craig A. Jones, USMC

When thinking about your next role in the civilian workforce think about the core competencies you have honed during your service time. Titles will not match up and that is okay. We know that and you cannot control that. However, what you can control is the way you break down the job you're seeking and the jobs you have had. Think about the skills it took to do your previous roles. Then match those skills up to what the employer is requesting. If you can show the potential employer that you have the skills they are requesting and how you have been successful at those in the past they will be more interested in getting you to the table, the interview, to talk further.

Realize you have the knowledge, skills, and experiences you need (within reason) for your next chapter. Go out there and show everyone. As an example, if you wanted to be a project manager. There is no rank of project manager in the military but think about the skills of a great project manager like communication, problem solving, and leadership. Show how you have accomplished those skills in previous roles across various titles by giving the employer the what, the how, and the result. If it is easier, break down the processes you have been through and how that relates to the processes the potential employer is asking you to carry out. Then break that down into skills.

LL #68: Build your brand.

Craig A. Jones, USMC

Your brand matters! Build it and maintain it often. What is this you say? The way folks see you showing up within the community. Are you engaged? Where are you? How do you engage? Do you help others? Are you portraying yourself in a good light?

Nowadays employers will seek you out on the various digital platforms. For a lot of businesses this means LinkedIn. When they "visit" you on the platform how will they "see" you? Will they see something that matches what you have submitted to them? Will they like what they see? Will they recognize you from past engagement? It is vastly important that you start building this out early. Your brand is never finished. You must maintain your brand, especially digitally, often, and continuously. Doing so will allow you to shine amongst the dull and this will add to your overall value and the value an employer will see you bring to them.

Sound daunting? It does not have to be. Follow the lead of others in your role, industry, and your desired companies. You will quickly realize who is doing branding well and whom is not.

LL #69: Build relationships.

Craig A. Jones, USMC

Networking is great. Having a large network is also great. Ask yourself though, do you have great relationships? You must build and maintain great relationships. You should start this early and maintain those closer relationships often. By building authentic relationships you are in essence creating a network of champions. This network of champions will certainly aide in your future success and be vital to both you and those you help.

Have the right expectations. These relationships are like fine wine. They will not happen overnight, and they may not be at their peak benefit for some time. Now, you may get lucky and have a short-term payoff, but do not go into it thinking that is the norm or try to treat each person like they have and will give something to you now. Foster them. Enjoy them. Your time will come and as done to you ... you will be that someone to someone else.

LL #70: Certify your skills.

Craig A. Jones, USMC

A certification is an official document attesting to a status or level of achievement. By obtaining a certification you are showing corporate America that you have the knowledge, skills, and experience within that profession. Certifications come in all sorts of shapes and sizes and thus hold different weightings with potential employers. You will do yourself a favor in seeking the right certification/s.

The right certification will differ depending on role, industry, and company. If there is much unknown into which certification a particular employer will value, start broader. For example, if you are seeking a role as an agile project manager, Project Management Institute's Agile Certified Practitioner (PMI-ACP) certification. This certification covers many agile methodologies and will certify you with such competencies.

Once within a company you may find they value one methodology over the other. You can then obtain a more specific certification in that methodology. Look for the certifications that companies are requesting within their job postings for your desired role/s and for ones that have education and experience requirements. Being certified will certainly help you to stand out among your peers and will give civilian employers a better opportunity to understand what value you bring to them.

LL #71: Organization, structure, and adaptability.

Kevin A. Knight, US Army Reserves ("USAR")

There are many factors and traits that make veterans attractive job candidates. Some of the traits my organization has expressed they seek, and noticed with me, is my ability to provide organization and structure to the projects I am running and the ability to adapt quickly with little to no push back.

During my transition into a civilian project manager role with my current organization, it has been mentioned by seniors, peers, operational management, and project team members how much they appreciate the attention to detail and organization I bring with the projects I am running. To me, I am simply doing what I feel is needed and right to move forward and meet the expectations demanded of me. I ask questions and seek verification when there is uncertainty, ensuring all parties are on the same page. I also document and provide meetings notes throughout the duration of projects, allowing team members the opportunity to reference back from previous conversations to get a full understanding of any issues or concerns currently holding up progress.

This has been extremely beneficial for management to look back on to understand where and what the issues are with any project being held up, providing them a strong foundation to present to executives.

Another big trait my organization likes is my ability to adapt and adjust to changes quickly. They provide me with an overview of the change and I simply adapt and continue to drive onward with my daily tasks while implementing the change. Management expects some push back or extensive explanation needed but have expressed several times this is not the case with me.

The above traits are all inherent traits I have obtained during my time in the military, making me the professional I am today. Organizations appreciate the structure and organization veterans bring to the table. Management also appreciates our ability to adapt quickly to changes with little to no resistance.

LL #72: Our Military is the best in the world...until transition time.

Nick Roberge, USMC

Our military is the best in the world. Period. This is not just because we have the best people, but because we take the time to provide in-depth and thorough education, training, and leadership opportunities to those individuals so that they can perform their jobs to the best of their abilities. When these individuals are employed as a team, they learn from each other's experiences and become a force multiplier towards a common goal. Often this is accomplishing whatever mission they may have been assigned. There is a sense of unity and bonding, a sense of achieving something bigger than themselves, all of which creates a real sense of a clear and concise purpose.

This is not done overnight. It takes many years of unit training, NCO academies, Professional Military Education, On the Job Training, and opportunities to fill roles of responsibilities to that of the next higher rank. We do an unbelievable job of turning civilians, often right out of high school or college, into highly functioning service members that make the highest functioning teams.

What we do not do very well is to take that same mentality, time, and energy to prepare our service members for civilian life. We go to a week-long transition class where they flood you with resume writing, how to navigate a job application, how you may have to dress, how to speak a few sentences without F bombs, and if there's enough time, maybe how to interview and follow up with a recruiter. But it is only a week. Hopefully, you plan to go twice about a year apart.

Sure, you have those few who retire, who were already working closely with a civilian team, and they get hired into a well-paying position doing the same thing in the same office. That is simply not the norm. For someone who has never applied for a job in the now digital world, it can be daunting. I remember reading a ton of job descriptions and simply did not know what the job entailed. Then there are the hours of resume tailoring with 50 different formats to pick from, plus include those keywords to get past the computer, and still somehow gain the attention within seven seconds that the average recruiter spends looking at them. There is still the interview, answering and asking the right questions, salary negotiations, the list goes on. This is all just how to land a job.

I would say the biggest thing to help figure everything out during your transition is to understand the language barrier between what you did in the military and how this relates to your future civilian employment. While there are many obvious differences in what the military may do, there are many types of jobs that are nearly the same in the civilian sector. We simply say it differently. Once you realize that the time you "led a squad to overcome obstacles, defeated the enemy, and achieved your objective", you may understand better how to "organize a sales or marketing team to outwit the competition in order to increase company profit margins".

There are dozens of other examples, but once you understand that a "Key Player" in the military is the same as a "Stakeholder" on the civilian side, keep expanding your vocabulary and just get the basic ideas down. You can always ask for help with the harder areas later, especially if you can utilize the awesome power of the veteran network. If you can apply the military's crawl-walk-run method to your transition the same way you were trained when you were in, you will undoubtedly be just as if not more successful than before.

LL #73: When is a good time to start preparing for transition?

Adam Reed, USN

When is it time to start preparing for your transition out of the military? The answer is yesterday! There is so much that goes into the military transition that preparation should happen several years prior to the decision to retire or simply getting out after your first or second tour. As professionals in the United States Military, we constantly strive to achieve the highest degree of readiness and ensure that our team is ready to face the fight.

However, there is a concurrent life that continues on as we progress throughout our military journey and that is our own personal development. As we hone our craft in the military, we need to be conscious about how we educate our minds while we are still active duty to ensure we provide ourselves with options when we begin the transition journey. Asking yourself what you want to do following your military career is the foundation of the transition process. If you know you want to continue doing project management then get your degree in project management.

Moreover, never settle, continue to set new goals, learn new things, and seek out more certifications that makes you marketable. The conundrum is finding harmony between your investment to the military, your personal growth and family.

I started my military transition 15 months prior to my separation date. I have a Master's in Logistics and Supply Chain Management, Lean Six Sigma Black Belt and I have my PMP. The first thing I did was determine where I wanted to live. Easily enough, my family wanted to stay in Jacksonville, Florida so that eliminated a major stressor immediately. I then asked myself where I could see myself working at in the Jacksonville metro area.

My initial list comprised of 30 companies that were reputable and have a firm foundation in the area. Determining who would be the best fit for me began with looking at current job openings on LinkedIn and ensuring that I meet the qualifications on the job post. In addition, I read about the company to determine if it was a culture fit for me. Once I reduced my list down to 10, I reached out to Vets at those companies to discuss life at that company.

One of the greatest takeaways from my military transition is never underestimate the power of the veteran network!!! There is a social media culture that vets will help other vets during their transition. What each person experiences during this time is not something that is entirely yours, many people before you have experienced the exact same emotional stress and uncertainty, reach out and glean the knowledge that is available to you.

When I was able to rank the companies I wanted to pursue, networked with Vets, and increased my LinkedIn connections I began to compile all my yearly evaluations. I started to translate my Naval career from military jargon to a story that captures my achievements in a way that someone that has no military experience can understand. Then its practice, practice, and practice. Once you initiate your request for retirement start planning out all the things that you will need for example a resume, LinkedIn profile or certifications.

As you start executing your plan be vigilant with monitoring your progress and controlling any variation in your plan if you discover new things you need to add. Make the necessary changes and keep moving forward. Ultimately, all this should culminate with finding a job and moving on to bigger and better things.

Warning, it can never be overstated the necessity of building your brand on social media. LinkedIn gives you a medium to establish yourself and to reach a greater population of talent acquisition professionals. Find your passion and talk about it. If you learned something about the VA medical process, share it! As we learn new things during this time, it is critical that we pay it forward and guarantee the message is passed on the next wave of transitioning vets. This brings me to current day, I have the education, I have professional certifications, I have networked and prepared for my upcoming interviews.

So, what is next?

I will carry the confidence that 20 years of military service has given me to execute the mission! Do I have everything figured out, absolutely not! I will continue to learn, seek out other Vets and continue to move forward. I still am afraid and uncertain but with the time spent preparing I know I can do this and what I am feeling will only fuel my determination and lastly, I can count on my fellow Vets for support!

LL #74: Tools for transitioning veterans - corporate culture.

Philip Hicks, USAF

The corporate culture of any organization creates additional complexity and ambiguity when transitioning from the military to a civilian career.

One strategy is to listen closely to what the hiring supervisor or interviewer is telling you through the interview. Of course, the demeanor and personality of the interviewer determine how this information is revealed. Are they asking questions that relate to the current problems they are experiencing? Do they freely talk about how interactions occur in the workplace between subordinates, peers, and superiors? Taking notes here can really pay dividends.

Additionally, at the appropriate time in the interview, you may be able to ask questions of the interviewer to gain additional pointed insight into the corporate culture.[21]

---

[21] https://www.linkedin.com/pulse/tools-transitioning-veterans-philip-hicks-p-e-m-same/

LL #75: What do I want to be when I grow up?

Philip Hicks, USAF

The next phase for me was to determine what I wanted to do for a living. While I had a variety of skills and abilities the Air Force had prepared me for while on active duty, I needed to distill the truth of those towards the civilian world. There are great tools on the internet for matching your Air Force specialty code (AFSC), functional area, or military occupational specialty (MOS) with civilian termed skills and abilities. However, they do not help you decide what you enjoy doing for a living.

By searching through my background and past job assignments, I was able to discern what I seemed to enjoy doing and excel at accomplishing. This did not happen in one sitting or over a week. This took many months of directed thought processing with multiple versions pushed out in different resumes and formats. I do not think I actually got it down until about three months before my terminal leave and eight to ten resume versions.

Determining what you want to be when you grow up is probably the most important first step to looking for a job. By defining what you enjoy doing and can be successful at, you are now beginning to define your future. Marrying the current skills and abilities to the next job is liberating because I started to envision myself in the position and roles in the future.[22]

22   https://www.linkedin.com/pulse/20141024143510-168102092-my-military-retirement-journey/

LL #76: Rehearse for success.

Philip Hicks, USAF

The military trains everyone to prepare for execution of any operation, project, program, etc. The job search was no different. One of the major items in the preparation was practicing or rehearsing what I planned to accomplish.

The 10 - 15 interviews were my initial rehearsal. I had a list of answered interview questions from my transition class and was able to expand upon them from a recruiting agency I was involved with. Each interview regardless of my overall interest in the position was a chance to practice my interview techniques. Answering potential interview questions well before going on the interviews turned out to be invaluable.

Phone interviews were the easiest. I had my resume and pre-answered interview questions electronically or in hard copy. I never recited and do not recommend delivering your remarks by reading directly from the prepared answers. Having the answered questions in front of you for the phone interview helps to kick-off your response by providing the topic you want to cover. Finish using your own thoughts and tie back to discussions from the interview.

Face-to-face interviews were definitely more challenging. I wore my best suit to the interviews and had to create habits for storing items in my pockets for easy access or not to cause bulges. Sitting in front of one to four recruiters and/or hiring authorities who are determining your potential for future employment can be unnerving. Again, answering the questions prior to the interview proved indispensable by preparing me mentally to be ready for the inevitable curve balls the interviewers presented.

The questions I was asked during the interviews are irrelevant. What is important is the rehearsal (answering sample questions, wearing the clothing, conduct and pacing, etc.) prior to the interviews for the jobs that I really wanted.[23]

---

[23]   https://www.linkedin.com/pulse/20141024143510-168102092-my-military-retirement-journey/

LL #77: Stress or less stress?

Mark Giles, USAF

Excitement, fear, sadness, joy, relief. These are just few of the emotions that a person experiences during their transition from the military to a civilian life. While every person's experience is unique, do not believe that you will escape a varying range of emotions. To put it simply, transition from the military is nothing short of an extremely stressful time for not only the military member, but his or her family as well. There is NO "magic pill" that will change this reality.

Questions such as do I move my family to a different geographic location? Do I change my profession from that of which I have been trained to perform while serving in the military? How long will it take for me to find sufficient employment? How do I cover healthcare expenses? Do I buy or rent a home? What type of garments do I need in my wardrobe now that I no longer will wear a uniform to my place of work?

The list of questions and uncertainties go on and on placing a great deal of pressure with no end in sight. When we boil down these "stressors" to a common thread, many of the issues can be resolved by gaining meaningful employment.

The good news is that there are actions that transitioning military members can take to this stressful experience. One such action is to educate yourself in a profession that is in high demand and document the experience gained as a manager and leader in the United States military. I am not talking about going to school and spending untold amounts of time in a classroom to obtain a degree. A college degree can help with certain job opportunities. I would not discourage anyone from pursuing a college education if that would help that person achieve their professional goals.

However, in today's corporate environment, certifications are taking a more prominent role. Not only does a certificate document classroom education but it also documents the experience that you have gained over years and maybe decades of military service. For example, a Project Management Certification such as Project Management Professional (PMP) is a highly sought after credential and is a "flag" used by corporate recruiters on the hunt to fill countless positions requiring experience in project management, budget, scheduling, risk management, team building, and a number of other skills that we all gain in military service no matter what career field we are trained. Gaining a certification requires each of us to work through our fear of failing, believe in ourselves and our abilities as well as select a course of action that will put us on a path to achieve our goal.

Vets2PM specializes in helping military members/veterans complete certification classroom requirements, document experience, prepare for and pass the certification exam, celebrate your achievements, prepare you for employment with a Project Management centric resume, and even match you with a perspective employer. The stress that I experienced in transition from the military, while still quite significant, was mitigated by finding and utilizing the help that the Vet2PM staff offered. Because of the PMP certification, a recruiter pulled my profile/resume, and resulted in a job offer before my retirement date.

In fact, I had to negotiate with the company to allow me the time that I needed with my family before beginning work in my civilian position. Are you looking at transitioning from the military? Does the prospect of change cause you overwhelming stress? My advice is not about the total elimination of stress, it is about reducing that stress so that you can focus on other things. Deal those stressors like you did everything else in your military career. Take the first step and meet the challenge head on. Utilize your education and certification benefits. Go get that project management certification! It is a gift to yourself that you will never regret.

LL #78: Veteran technical skills.

Reid Denson, USA

Overcome the idea that you are lacking technical skills. I believe many transitioning Vets feel very confident in the "soft skills", but do not consider the technical skills they developed in service, other than equipment or IT systems they may have used. What many vets are missing is industry-specific technical skills or experience. Project management, planning, scheduling, logistics, training management, are all technical skills. While the soft skills have served me well, in my experience, the feedback I've received for any job offers or follow up interviews indicated that it was my certification or ability to plan and manage a schedule that made me competitive in the eyes of employers.

So, take inventory of your technical and your soft skills. Utilize your education and certification processes to validate and hone those technical skills.

LL #79: What I learned from the...

Kaylin Haywood, USAF

What I learned from the Air Force is that relationships are important. Do not rely upon emails. Build relationships. Learn your environment and function within it; balance with improving process but understand why they do what they are doing first. Take initiative and be adaptable. Do not wait for someone else to solve the problem--adapt to situations and move, work around, or push through obstacles to achieve goals. But do it. Most importantly, ensure you cover peoples' back and have people covering your back.

What I learned from my transition is that what I learned from the Air Force applied to a successful transition from the military but just like in the military you need someone who has your six.

Transitioning out of the military can leave you feeling abandoned, frustrated, and a little depressed. TAP class is overwhelming—who can even start to figure out the VA when you cannot even explain your career. All of the articles and advice on interviewing, getting your resume past computer screeners, learning to answer interview questions. Military do not have interview experience and now find themselves up against people who have interviewed for jobs for the past 20 plus years.
It is hard to explain military skills and experience. Writing and rewriting a resume and translating it to a LinkedIn profile. Every bit of it steals your confidence, makes you doubt your abilities and wonder how those years in the military could mean nothing to the private sector.

You need someone who has your six through this process. It is like the first day in the military--a fire hose of information and even though you are all speaking the same language ... you discover you are not. It is not a weakness to admit you need someone to fly your six, in the military it is required. It is the same when you transition. You need a real person, not a link to a website, not a video, not a webinar...you need a battle buddy. You would not deploy without training; you do not get into the cockpit without learning from experts...do not make one of the biggest transitions of your life without training and experts.

Media builds a story in the mind of many about what someone in the military can and cannot do and what skills you have. Translating what you did for our country requires someone who knows the environment, an interpreter, in order to ensure skills, experiences, and leadership make sense to the private sector.

As you move to this new environment, do not expect the interviewer, hiring manager to solve the problem of understanding your worth. You need to adapt and overcome the challenge but just like in the military you do not have to do it on your own. Supported by skills and experience, armed with energy and passion for what you did, and with Vet2PM on your six, you will succeed.

LL #80: Transitioning from military to civilian life.

Heide Gabriella, USN

Let go of doubt and have faith in yourself. There is always a reason and a purpose why this transition is happening. The universe closes one chapter to guide you into the next chapter of your journey. That next chapter will lead you to the next step in your life's purpose of discovering the joy you have been desiring.
The universe will get you there, one step at a time. It may not happen overnight and could take months or years. Sometimes the transition takes a long time for you to realize the person you are meant to be and bring it here into reality.

What truly works in this transition is trusting in yourself, having faith and finding happiness during your growth. Know that you are taking the right direction on your own path to reach the success that is necessary for you. You know what you need to do to get to the next level. And you have a multitude of veteran resources to help you along the way. It may mean taking a higher education, a new job, updating your resume or opening a business but there are many organizations looking to help you through it all. Trust in yourself and take that leap of faith. You are not alone.

LL #81: Disagreement is not disrespect.

Bruce Townshend, USAR

After the conclusion of the REFORGER (Return of Forces to Germany) in 1989, which turned out to be the very last incarnation of that exercise, I was honored to take part in a conversation with our battalion commander after we conducted our official AAR (After Action Review) of the battalion's performance in the maneuvers. I had just left my position as a platoon leader in a Military Police company and been assigned as the S-2 (security and intelligence) staff officer for a Military Police battalion in southern Germany.

The battalion commander, a lieutenant colonel, asked the junior officers to stay behind for an hour or so in order to get to know us better and to offer us a chance to speak to him without the filters of the more senior officers and staff as buffers or barriers. He asked us again our impressions of the battalion's missions, successes, and challenges during REFORGER and then he asked us, each in turn, for what we thought personally could have been done better. Not a single one of the dozen or so of us offered up anything useful and most of our comments were simply rehashed interpretations of what our company commanders and senior staff members had already stated.

Sensing our reluctance, he gave us another chance. With a rather wry smile on his face he gently chastised us for being "too nice" and for not giving him our honest evaluations and offering forthright personal perspectives. And then he said something have never forgotten, and never will. He said to us "Disagreement is not disrespect". He was looking me right in the eye as he spoke those words.

I cannot speak for the rest of the young lieutenants and very junior captains at the table, but that statement was a like a thunderclap crashing over my head. The commander explained what he meant and told us that we should never be afraid to voice a legitimate concern or an alternate point of view, especially when asked to do precisely that, so long as it was done respectfully and tactfully. He admitted that he knew the by-the-book answers to most of the missions with which our battalion was tasked by he often lacked the perspective of other officers and Soldiers, which he considered every bit as important as his own or those of his superiors. He further emphasized that disrespect is disrespect and that many in the military culture, especially those in leadership or supervisory positions, had forgotten that honest and forthright disagreement was not only necessary but desirable, and that good leaders both knew the difference and encouraged spirited discussions.

To this day, more than 30 years on, I could not have a higher level of respect for that battalion commander and how his wisdom guided my further career and positively affected my life.

I took that lesson with me throughout the rest of my military career, both in the active force and the reserve component, and have applied it liberally to every non-military government position and the private sector occupations I have held. I have had the honor to serve as a supervisor or in leadership positions many times since that day in September 1989, and I know that I do not have all the answers or know the best path forward in all circumstances. I know the difference between honest disagreement and disrespect or disdain. The lesson has served me well and kept me from being the victim of my own hubris and arrogance many times.

LL #82: Preparation and perseverance carry the day.

Timothy R. McCardle, USMC

Or, Things I Wished I Had Learned in Military Transition Assistance Program Class...

I transitioned from active duty in 2010 after serving twenty-six years in our US Marine Corps. My transition was family-driven and quick. I left active duty with the minimum notice that the Marine Corps allows- four months. I earned my MBA degree nine months before transitioning. While my transition has been ultimately successful for both me and my family, it was very stressful. There are a couple things I wish I would have learned in military transition assistance program class are as follows:

"It is ok to change jobs". In the Marine Corps, I transferred duty stations every three to four years. Many civilians change jobs at a similar interval. Changing jobs is possibly the only way you will move up, especially if you are in a small organization. Veterans initially change jobs at a higher rate than civilians as they discover their job preferences.

"Live in a familiar locale". If you do not plan to live in the same area where you left active duty, select a place close to family, friends, or someplace you and your family know. You will need a solid support network as will your family.

"Stick to your core competency". Look for your first job in a similar field that you worked in on active duty. The transition will be less stressful for you. You can always change jobs after you are stable.

"Stick to your values". You will be disappointed in the lack of honor, moral courage, commitment, and work ethic of civilians you encounter who never served. Do not compromise your integrity.

"Be a lifelong learner". Whatever occupation you choose, look to learn as much as you can to be the subject matter expert. Advanced degrees and professional certifications such as PMP, LSSBB, and SHRM-CP are examples. "Know yourself and seek self-improvement" from the USMC Leadership Principles applies.

Whether serving for four years or twenty-six years, military transition is a challenge. You are up to the challenge. Preparation and perseverance carry the day.

LL #83: The big reset – rank is gone and that is OK.

Ray K. Ragan, USAR

You are about to take perhaps one of the biggest professional steps since you met your drill sergeant. Transitioning to the civilian workforce will be huge culture shock, perhaps even more consequential than when you were told to "beat your face" in basic training. One of the biggest culture shocks for transitioning service members is realizing that whatever rank you wore is gone and that is true with everyone else in the room. You can no longer glance around the room and figure out who outranks who.

In the civilian workplace, it is a lot more nuanced than rank hierarchy. Sure, there are organizations that maintain a very hierarchical structure, but they are being replaced by flatter organizations where senior leaders do not make every decision. This is especially true in tech companies, where merit is more valuable than title. This can be challenging for some and a blessing for others. Now, as a civilian, you are more likely to be judged by your contributions than your title. Remember that. Consciously remind yourself that whatever your rank was that your team and the team of teams are judging you on how you contribute and treat others. Propel the team to greatness and you will do great in your civilian career – fortunately, the military prepared you for this already.

MISSION TIPS:
- Consciously separate yourself from rank and role in civilian settings, listen to the merit of ideas to prepare and solve for the future.
- Be prepared to challenge positions of senior leaders with data and evidence to put the entire team closer to reality.
- Cultivate a culture where you succeed through the team and the team's success is your success.

LL #84: Resume translation including mapping rank to civilian job level.

Daniel Kaminske, USAF

The Air Force Transition Program did assist me in creating a resume which translated some of my military accomplishments into relatable civilian terms. However, this did not provide me the knowledge or insight to be able to develop an effective resume for a civilian position that was remotely equivalent to my capabilities I had successfully demonstrated while on active duty. As an NCO I was acclimated in managing multiple employees and projects simultaneously.

Vets2PM helped me realize the parallels of this experience to IT Project Management. They provided me tools, templates and face to face guidance which enabled me to translate my Air Force experience into terms which directly translated to very specific Project Manager job positions I was interested in. This was the steppingstone I was missing in getting the attention of civilian employers based on my very similar work experience I obtained in the military.

LL #85: The importance of the PMP certification even for non-veterans.

Daniel Kaminske, USAF

I first learned of the project management field in college before entering into the Air Force. What I did not learn during that time is how vital it is to obtain the PMP Certification if you are interested in pursuing a career in that field. Now that I have been working as an IT Project Manager for a few years after separating from the military I have seen firsthand how much this certification is in demand. I wish I had gotten it as I was transitioning out of the Air Force. This would have made it much easier for me to land a well-paying and prestigious job right away.

Having the PMP Certification before I started my career as a project manager would have spring boarded me into much more senior and higher paying roles much sooner. The final point I want to highlight is that this certification holds a lot of weight for civilian jobs even in most careers outside of project management as well. It has been well worth the investment for me!

LL #86: Corporate America is different.

Craig Washburn, USN

From the moment I stepped off the bus at the Naval Training Command in Orlando, Florida on Jan 3, 1991, the lessons in chain of command began. For a nineteen-year-old surf rat that did not like to be told what to do, let me just say, it was an adjustment. It took everything in me not to do or say something stupid. I did not understand the method behind the madness.

Two weeks into boot camp, we were awakened abruptly by our company commanders. Everyone scrambled to get to our assigned positions by our bunks and we stood at attention. The next words that were spoken, put everything in perspective. "Today, the United States of America, is at war with Iraq. Most of you will immediately deploy upon completion of boot camp or your technical schools. What you learn here may be the difference whether you live or die".

The rest of the morning consisted of lectures on why chain of command and attention to detail matter. In the military, we follow orders. We expect our troops to follow orders. There are consequences if orders are not followed. It is engrained in us.

Fast forward six years as I began my first real career in corporate America. I left the military as an E-5 and was fortunate enough to earn a supervisory role within the first few months at my first company. It was not that difficult. I just did what was asked of me and did it to the best of my ability. What I quickly found out as I stepped into the new role was following directions (orders) without pushback was not the norm.

I was extremely excited and honored to be entrusted to lead my new team in pursuit of the company's objectives. Each day I would rally the team in the morning, layout out our objectives for the day, give individual assignments and get everyone off to work. After the first week in role though, my excitement turned to utter stress. That Friday, I was called into my manager's office. Apparently, I was being "too firm" with my team and it was affecting their morale. I was caught completely off guard. He explained "as a leader in the the corporate world, you have to inspire people to want to do their job". I remember leaving that meeting in complete shock.

I wish I could tell you that I was able to make an immediate shift into the new, softer approach, but it took a while. It required me to rewire circuits in my brain that were hard wired. This was a new culture that was foreign and did not make much sense to me. I knew though, if I were going to succeed, I needed to improvise and adapt. I committed myself to learning through mentorships and a lot of reading on self-development and leadership. I tell this story not to scare my transitioning brethren or to berate corporate America, but to help you prepare mentally for your new world and to help you succeed.

LL #87: Put your ego in the desk drawer.

Craig Washburn, USN

One of the hardest lessons for many (me included) to learn during the transition to civilian careers is how long and how challenging it can be to first, land your dream job and then, move up the corporate ladder. There are few other times in your life that can beat your ego into the dirt like transition if you let it.

In our new world of technology, getting a resume in front of the right people is challenging. We think that if we apply to a position online that someone will see our resume. Knowing all that we bring to the table, we expect to have someone call us within a few days begging us for an interview. Unfortunately, that scenario could not be farther from the truth.

The reality is, our resumes go into a database along with all the other resumes submitted for every other position at that company. The recruiters' type in key words to match candidates and experience with the open positions. Then they screen each resume to narrow down the field to who they want to interview. If your resume is not tailored to the job description, chances are it will never get looked at.

This revelation is not meant to scare you, but to prepare you mentally for what you are up against. The good news is, there are work arounds if you check your ego. I know most of us feel we are capable of accomplishing anything we set our minds to; all by ourselves. I have no doubt, that you can do this on your own, but I will submit to you that it will be much easier and much faster if you ask for help.

There are 43,000+ Veteran focused organization whose sole mission is to be a resource for you. Many of these organizations have people assigned to help Veterans with resume assistance, mock interviews, and job search techniques. There are also countless Veterans that would be willing to mentor you if you just ask for help. Do not be afraid to network with Veterans at the company you are targeting to learn more about the company, culture and what you should do to make yourself more marketable to the people reviewing resumes. If you do it right, that Veteran may just walk your resume down to the hiring manager.

Once you land in your new career, the next potential challenge many faces are expecting advancement within a defined period of time. In the military, career progression follows a defined progression. You put in your time, you do a few extras if you want, you take tests and when all the points add up above the promotion line, bingo. Who you know and how you are with office politics do not matter until you reach senior ranks. In the corporate world, they do not follow that model. Every company has different approaches to advancement.

To save you from sleepless nights, the best recommendation I can give is after you get settled and become competent in your new role, make your interest to grow with the company into positions of greater responsibility known to your immediate leadership. Ask for specific objectives you can work towards to prepare you for the next level. Be willing to work harder and longer than your peers and accomplish the objectives given to you.

Lastly, be patient. Sometimes budget, or other considerations you may not be aware of delay advancement. If you prove every day that you are going to do what it takes to help the company succeed, your efforts will be rewarded.

LL #88: Do not have unrealistic expectations from recruiters.

Cathy Miclat

What do I mean? Here's the scenario: You see a job posting you are interested in, you take time to make sure your resume is in line with the job requirements, you sweat over an appropriate cover letter, and you finally click 'Submit.' You begin checking your email every day for a response...Sure, you likely received the 'Thanks for submitting your resume' response that is system generated, but you are waiting for the reach out from a recruiter at the company who is excited to screen you for the job. And...you get crickets.

Why does this happen? Well, there are two sides to every story and the fact is that corporate recruiters are generally not rude at all, just often overwhelmed with balancing multiple positions and they are interested in filling the jobs for their hiring managers because that is what measures their success and the company's quotas. They are also scheduling phone screens, in person interviews, and managing these activities for several demanding hiring managers who are hiring for several positions. Their priority, unfortunately, is not to send you a letter saying that you do not match the job and why.

What can you do? First, do not take it personally. They are not trying to make you feel bad, they are just trying to keep their heads above water. And, from someone who has been in that industry for many years, the hardest thing a recruiter must do is tell someone no. They feel bad about it, so some likely avoid it at all costs; also, some candidates who receive a rejection want to begin an ongoing dialogue to show why they *are* the right person for the job. The recruiter just does not have time for that. This is simply a harsh reality. So, what can you do? I suggest follow up (if you have an email address) with the recruiter asking for an update, if there are any questions you can answer, or additional information you can provide, while reiterating your interest in the position. Then move on. There are other opportunities out there.

The moral of the story is this – recruiters may disappoint you more than they will surprise you; but they are a necessary part of the process. Applicant tracking systems seem like a black hole; but they are also a necessary part of the process. Understand that job search rejections are not personal. The effort of going through this process teaches you invaluable lessons about yourself, the companies you are applying for, how to network, and ultimately how to treat people when you are on the other side of the desk (which will happen).

Start early; look inward for your passion; research companies; build and use your network; ask for help; do not take it personally; and stay the course. It will work out and you will find that first or next great career in Corporate America.

LL #89: What is your career 'Gold'?

Garrik Dennis, USA

What is your career "gold?" Psychology professor and clinical psychologist Dr. Jordan Peterson reflects on the needed confrontation of one's "dragon" in order to secure their "gold" in life.

Veterans have a unique challenge in evolving from a meaning-inherent "pool" military career to the vast ocean of the CIVDIV, as the countless directions and opportunities are contrasted with an overwhelming sense of identity-loss. Boldly confront your identity and career dragons to get YOUR gold; know that your experience and leadership exposure is wildly valuable in the CIVDIV, and your personal identity can be healthily solidified external to your career choice.

This honorable battle can assuredly lead to personal and professional health, and ultimate victory as you journey through the sometimes-rough waters of transition and life.

LL #90: Fitness.

Garrik Dennis, US Army

Veterans. Fitness. Physical fitness. Prioritize it, for when it degrades, the affects you experience will be prioritizing YOU!

Keep the lineage you have with the military by staying in community and in fitness. The physiological and psychological effects can greatly and positively impact your day, and therefore the powerful influence you are capable of having on others in this life.

LL #91: Resisting change.

Garrik Dennis, US Army

No matter the challenge facing you in life, resisting change may only serve to exacerbate the potential discomfort that accompanies it. Consider embracing change and accepting that growth is sometimes preceded by pain. Like water, perhaps, continue moving to stay fresh; continue growing and evolving to stay healthy and fight the chaos of stagnation.

LL #92: The difference between a job and an occupation.

Joshua P. Frank, USA

When we leave the service, we look for a job. When we grasp the concept of life-long-learning, we gain an occupation.

More than twenty years ago, I left the military service and my first job was a project manager for a technology company. The translation of military experience into corporate value often involves project management (PM). This does not imply that every service member enters corporate America as a PM. It is however a common transition.

Nine times out of ten, your first position is a job. Will you stay at the first company for more than a year or two? Probably not. But the more you learn about the commercial market the stronger your skill set becomes and the more valuable you will be to other companies.

What many of us do not realize is that the difference between a job and an occupation is life-long-learning. Your military leadership experience, whether you were a team leader on an infantry squad, a warrant officer, or a company or field grade officer, your leadership experience is highly valued by corporate America. However, your first post-military position is likely to be a job. Your work ethic and desire to continually improve is what mentally and physically moves you into an occupation.

A job pays the bills. An occupation helps you raise a family and save for retirement. A job is clocking in from nine to five. An occupation provides financial independence.

An occupation provides you with the foundation for starting your own company, should you choose to do so.

Your experience in the military is highly desired by corporate America. If you want to grow, make more money, and be in the top 5% of your peer group, you need to continually widen your horizons and never stop learning.

Getting from a job to an occupation does not happen overnight. It takes time. It can take more than a year after leaving the service. Why? Because you need to embrace life-long-learning. This concept is more than a buzz-phrase or philosophical concept. It is truly how you catapult from your first post-military job into financial independence. So, what does this look like? It starts with a plan. Do you have a college degree? An associates or bachelors? If you do not have a degree, are you ready to better yourself? Perhaps college is not for you and you need to obtain a specific certification? Have you joined the right associations for your industry? Do you have two or more mentors to help you transition?

Whether you are getting ready to leave the military, have just arrived in corporate America, or you've been out of the military for years, what can you do right now to improve your knowledge of your market and industry? Should you go back to school for a degree or some other certification? No matter what you decide to do, your success will be heavily reliant on always improving your capabilities. The difference between a job and an occupation is life-long-learning.

Something to think about.

LL #93: Resetting your brain for entrepreneurial success.

Michael LeJeune, USA

Regardless of how long you have been in the military or what branch you were in; you have been trained to think a certain way. All of that training probably suited you well in uniform. Only some of it will benefit you moving forward.

One of the first lessons you will learn as an entrepreneur is that you need to think for yourself and trust your gut. There are no procedures or operations manuals that clearly define how to be successful or even what that looks like for you. A lot of people will try to tell you what success means to them. Your first objective as an entrepreneur is to define what success means to YOU. Your definition of success can and should look very different than everyone else you talk to. Otherwise, you are living someone else's dream and that often means living by their rules.

Before you jump into your entrepreneurial journey, I recommend a hard reset to your thinking. Go away for a weekend by yourself with nothing more than a notebook. Plan some quiet time to think about what you want to be when you grow up, what your core value are, what your ideal life looks like, and the type of business you want to build. Remove ALL the rules! Do not throw them away, just put them aside. Then as you build your dream life, slowly integrate YOUR rules of the game back into your plan.

LL #94: Learn how to sell anything.

Michael LeJeune, USA

The single greatest skill you can learn for ANY type of business is how to sell. Money may not buy you happiness, but it pays the bills. Just about any problem in business can be solved by bringing in additional revenue. If you need new equipment, bring in the sales to pay cash for it. If you need to hire new folks, bring in additional sales to pay for it. In a jam financially? Go sell something to get out of the jam! Shall I go on?

The point is that sales drive literally everything for a company. No sales equal no company. Entrepreneurs often go wrong by focusing on their product/service, processes, and other intangibles. These things are important, but do not matter if you cannot sell the products/services you provide.

So, what do you do? Get some sales training. There is an infinite number of options. You can attend webinars, buy books, get coaching, or get a mentor. Another great way to learn how to sell is to take an entry level sales position. A lot of big companies have great sales training that you can get paid to attend. You may even do like I did and do ALL of the above.

Over time, you will develop your own style of selling. You will also realize that you are ALWAYS fine-tuning your approach to get better. The better you get at sales, the more you make. If you are REALLY good at sales, you can train others how to sell your products/services and duplicate yourself many times over. That is the secret to scalability.

LL #95: Branding yourself as an expert.

Michael LeJeune, USA

The age-old question. Do I brand myself or my company? My answer. You brand them both! The most common argument for branding your company is that you do not want it to be all about you and someday you want it to run without you. That is great. It is also a long-term vision. But let me throw a wrench in that plan. Let us say you only brand your company. Five years down the road the company is a huge success and you sell it. Then what? How do you leverage that success for your next business? The truth is that it is going to be difficult if no one knows your name. The truth is that you will be starting from scratch to either build your brand or the new company brand.

So, what if you brand yourself while branding your company? What would happen if five years down the road you still decide to sell the business? The good news is that this time, YOU are well known in the industry. If you've branded yourself properly, you are known as a top expert in your field, you are being followed by thousands of people on social media, you probably have a bestselling book, and key players in your market know who you are.

In this second scenario, you will EASILY move into your next venture. In fact, people will probably be begging you to join them in order to leverage YOU to grow an existing brand. But even if you start a new company from scratch, you still have YOUR BRAND and YOUR FOLLOWING that you can leverage to make the transition.

LL #96: Adapt and overcome.

Dana L. White, US Air Force Reserve ("USAFR")

I come from a family with a military background and I personally have a CIV-MIL-CIV background as an Air Force reservist in a Combat Search and Rescue Unit. At one point, the adjustment back to civilian life was challenging because of the stark differences in the level of discipline and order. My internal reactions to various civilian situations were separating me further and further from navigating efficiently in the civilian world. However, I have realized that being active in the military equipped me with both transferrable skills and a strong community of support.

Although, I started my career as a civilian in various engineering disciplines, being in the military for about a decade made the transition back into the civilian workforce pretty tough. Rather than going back to work in corporate America, I chose entrepreneurship. After my overseas deployment in 2014, I started a marketing agency and found that balancing active duty and starting a company from the ground up was a unique challenge.

However, through my military training I have learned to operate by the mantra that when it comes to accomplishing a mission, no is not a choice and failure is not an option. I was determined to make it all work, so I found business networks to help me achieve my goals.

My strong networks have helped the pieces all come together. Through my networks, I have been able to develop mutually beneficial relationships with other entrepreneurs where we are able to help each other and learn from each other. The key is to make purposeful connections to establish valuable relationships that promote personal and professional growth. I was able to jumpstart my network through local business affiliations and Veterans groups. Although I was dreading it, I threw myself into the networking mix, met a lot of great people, and propelled my business forward.

On a personal level, networking has allowed me to connect with fellow Veterans as well as learn more patience and strategies to deal with various personality types, communication styles, and work habits. Regarding my business, I was able to interact with the community, get to know clients, and gauge my operating environment. Since people like to do business with those that they know, like, and trust building that strong network allowed others to get to know my business and me. It also allowed people to see the core values of integrity, service, and selflessness that have been instilled by the military.

The biggest lesson learned is to not be resistant to change. Adapt and overcome.

LL #97: A Veteran Inspired.

Dave Esra, USAR

VETERAN INSPIRATION…THEY SAID
GET CERTIFIED AND CREDENTIALED….THEY
SAID
CIVILIAN PROFESSIONAL DEVELOPMENT….THEY
WERE RIGHT.

I got the recommendation to attend the Vets2PM course at the local PMI chapter after PCSing back from Europe. For a second career, I knew that Project Management was in my wheelhouse after 20 years military service that included two command positions and multiple S-3 Operations positions. Doc Wright verified that during our first session. He said that veterans make great Project Managers. I wanted to lead teams again and make an impact. Little did I know how right Doc Wright would be (see what I did there?).

The course did exactly what they said it would. It provided the translation from military lingo to corporate / business lingo. The tools, techniques, and skills the Army teaches to its leaders, such as the Military Decision-Making Process and Troop Leading Procedures translate directly into the PMBOK knowledge areas and phases (Inputs, Tools and Techniques, and Outputs). Just as I stuck to the

Army Operations Process as a Junior Officer and Staff member, I was about to hold onto that PMBOK like a PM Ranger Handbook.

I took the Vets2PM course twice. No, I wasn't trying to get my money's worth, I just wanted to pass the test the first time. Thanks to the level of service offered by Doc's team, I celebrated my PMP certification in Aug 2016. Immediately I got my first IT Project Management position. I wasn't an expert in the IT field, but I was prepared, because I had the Project Management tools and techniques the Vets2PM team gave me. I knew the PMBOK, and my plan was to stick to the basics, the same way I stuck to the Army basic OPORDER process. It worked.

There is always the caveat, that you never see the textbook version in the real world. That's totally true, but what I saw was worse than that. I worked for multiple PMOs in several industries. Without fail, the PMOs would lack basic standards and best practices provided by PMI. Just like writing an Operations Order, I would be the only PM developing the standard PM Plans: Scope, Schedule, Quality, Change management, etc. As mentioned, I try to keep to the basics. I always brought my PM bag of tricks: a

RAID log, a charter template, Project Management Plans, and Team Ground Rules (THANKS DOC, that one is a real gem!)

Well it got noticed that my projects were always healthier, more responsive, and consistently delivered value. When asked about this by leadership, I showed them the standard tools. I told my leaders how a new PM could step into my project and easily take things over based off my documentation. Remember the ITTOs? Output of updating PM documentation? Super important folks.

Within less than 2 years of getting my PMP certification, I was working as a Senior PM at a Fortune 100 company. Within 1 year of getting hired there, I was promoted to Lead PM. Then within 6 months of that, I was promoted to Director and asked to build and run a PMO for one of the Senior Executives.

My point here is not to brag (though pretty awesome huh!) My point is that I did all this by sticking to the basics. I had many occasions where other PMs and leaders told me, "we don't do PMI here"…"we do it the company way". I do believe that the organizational knowledge is important, but I do not think any company will ever see consistent successful project delivery without basic standards. Sound familiar...Basic Standards and Discipline from bootcamp?

Fortunately for us, PMI (Project Management Institute) makes it easy. They provide the best business practices along with the methodology and tools to run successful projects. By the way, those practices will keep you compliant if you are in a regulated environment.

You'll see all kinds of PMs in a career in Project Management. Some have excellent organizational skills, some are PowerPoint gurus, some brilliant academics, and some amazing leaders. It is the leadership part that no one trains better than the US Military. I often see prior military service PMs with a more complete set of qualities that are perfect for project management.

Remember when I mentioned that Doc Wright said the Vets make great PMs, well I actively recruit my PMs from the military. Now, one third of my team are Veterans. I am especially proud of our connection to the military and the level of experience and leadership they bring to the table. I now have a diverse team with a wealth of knowledge and expertise. We have consistently set the standard for our company, with multiple PMOs following our lead. We deliver excellence and consistent business value to our stakeholders.

So, they were right. I am inspired. I am inspired that proficiency in those basic PMI standards can lead to a successful (yes lucrative) civilian career. I am inspired to encourage my Veteran Brothers and Sisters to seek the PMP certification so that I can have them on my team, delivering excellence and building the future of project management culture. I'm inspired to serve in a project management leadership capacity, empowering project managers to do the right thing when it's the hard thing to do. I know that they will always have the courage to do so, especially those who had the courage to raise their hand and serve our great nation.

Doc, Cathy, and all the Vets2PM team, thank you for what you are doing for us. You are all great Americans, and I thank you for your service to our nation and to our Veterans.

LL #98: Forever brothers/sisters in arms.

Joe Pusz

VPMMA, the Veteran Project Manager Mentor Alliance, was formed to provide a platform for transitioning Servicemembers interested in Project Management careers to receive mentoring and guidance during the transition. As Co-Founder and a civilian who didn't serve, I wanted to be able to give back to those who have served us. Mentoring has a been an important aspect of my professional growth and I've been fortunate to be both a mentor and a mentee. My mentors have helped with career coaching, executive leadership skills, project management, personal learning and so much more. I've mentored project managers seeking professional guidance, transitioning Veterans and disadvantaged middle school girls. Whether a mentor or a mentee one thing has always been constant in my mentoring experiences – *building trust is a must*!

Once trust has been built between the mentor and mentee the real growth takes place as each is more open, direct, and targeted in the relationship. After several years of VPMMA I noticed something I had not experienced within any of my personal mentoring experiences.

There is an outpouring of support from Veterans to support other Veterans. The great majority of our Mentors within VPMMA are also Veterans. They have transitioned from their respective military careers and are now established project managers in the "Civ Div." They understand the challenges faced during the transition. They understand the cultural differences. They understand translation from military language to civilian terminology. They have been there and done that. Regardless of their military branch, the Veterans step up and volunteer to help their fellow Brothers and Sisters through the transition to a civilian career. There is an unspoken bond that allows for the trust to form quickly moving the relationship forward to value added activity.

I want to share a few messages we have received from Veterans who have signed up to be mentors in VPMMA so that you can read in their words how important it is for them to continue to serve.

"I have had great adventures rising to get where I am today. Every step of the way there is great men and women who have mentored and shaped my path. These selfless leaders have pushed me to my potential and then to keep going. Today, I look for opportunities to continue the tradition and build into others from my experience, insight, and knowledge. I love teaching and seeing the epiphany moment but mostly I love seeing people succeed. I am humbled when an opportunity presents itself and here, we are". Chris D. United States Air Force Veteran and VPMMA Mentor.

"Translating relevant military experience into functional corporate project management expectations is a key part of my job. I love highlighting the abilities that are exemplified within the military and how to leverage those skills to excel in new opportunities. I've been very fortunate to move from, essentially, the bottom of the totem pole with my company (a large construction company) into a mid-level executive within a few years, by simply staying true to my military training, experience, drive, and diligence. I would love the opportunity to help others succeed just the same". Aaron M. United States Army Veteran and VPMMA Mentor.

"I'm in the position to give back to my fellow veterans and project managers and would like to aide in others' success for a better future for all". Craig J. United States Marine Veteran and VPMMA Mentor.

"I'm a Navy vet who had to figure out the 'Vet Stone' on my own when I left service in 2005.[24] I wish this had been a resource in my TAPS class. I've been a project manager really since my first civilian job in 2005, and a certified PMP since April 2015". Katherine M. United States Navy Veteran and VPMMA Mentor.

The continued service from our mentors speaks to their character, dedication, and training to serve others. As Co-Founder of VPMMA my desire is to assist as many Veterans as possible during their transition. What I've found on this journey is how much I've learned from these Veterans. How important service is to one another and their community, and how strong the bond is between those who have served in the U.S. Military.

---

[24] "Vet Stone" is a concept developed by Doc Wright, to represent the translation of military experience into project management experience.

LL #99: Keep your grit.

Eric "Doc" Wright, USN & USARNG

Your transition will be difficult. You'll realize you didn't start early enough, plan enough, or know enough. However, just like anything you did during your military service, just keep putting one foot in front of the other, to make it to lunch, or back to post. Every DI goes home sometime! There'll be time to process, reflect, and adjust later, persevere now. Stay gritty!

How? With a positive mental attitude. You will succeed. Henry Ford once said, "If you think you will or if you think you won't, you're right either way".

LL #100: Venn it out!

Eric "Doc" Wright, USN & USARNG

One way to do this is to draw a two-bubble Venn diagram on a piece of blank paper, labeling the left bubble "Liked" and the right bubble "Disliked". Jot down as many items in each as you can, arriving at a list of things you like to do and that you liked about your service, and a list of things you don't like to do and didn't like about your service. Use this list while you read job descriptions, ignoring titles, companies, salaries, etc. Find descriptions you like, then look at those companies on LinkedIn and their respective company Web Sites.

LL #101: We are not islands.

Eric "Doc" Wright, USN & USARNG

According to the US Department of Veterans Affairs ("USDVA"), about two hundred thousand of our brothers and sisters in arms join us as veterans in the CIVDIV each year.[25] It is my opinion that since we are ahead of them on the path, we should reach back and help them advance. Guide them.

I can tell you from my own twelve years spent doing it without a guide, wandering lost in the job desert, it sucks! I can also tell you from many recent years spent being a guide to others, it is fulfilling, cathartic, and the right thing to do by them, ourselves, and our great Nation! Be your brother and sister's keeper. Please give them this book. Or buy them one if you would like to keep yours. We only took off the uniform, not our oaths.

Thank you.

Cheers!

---

[25] https://www.benefits.va.gov/transition/tap.asp

About Vets2PM

Vets2PM alumni manage project portfolios of $6.5+ Billion annually for over 620 agencies, non-profits, and Fortune 500 companies. With thousands trained and 502 PMP-certificate holders, Vets2PM is one of the nation's largest and fastest-growing PMP certification and placement companies in the country.

We help veterans streamline the transition from military to meaningful, lucrative post-service intra or entrepreneur careers by providing (1) training and credentialing, (2) project manager staffing and placement, (3) Project Management as a Service (PMaaS), i.e. project performance management and auditing, and (4) small business coaching. We excel, however, at delivering custom training solutions that ensure statutory compliance for government staffs, profitability for government contractors, and high civilian job market fit for veterans.

Vets2PM is a Department of Veterans Affairs certified Service-Disabled Veteran Owned Business, and a Department of Labor 2019 HIRE Vets Gold Award Winner in the Small Business category. We walk the talk.

Visit www.vets2pm.com today to get started down the path to your meaningful, lucrative post-service intra or entrepreneur career.

About the Veteran Project Manager Mentor Alliance

Doc Wright co-founded the Veteran Project Manager Mentoring Alliance (VPMMA) with Joe Pusz of the PMO SQUAD to provide project management mentoring access and national networking opportunities to our great Nation's military member, veteran, and spouse project managers, as well as veterans seeking to transition into civilian project management careers.

Please donate your time, expertise, and corporate donations/sponsorships today at: www.thevpmma.org.

Additionally, **please use smile.amazon.com** to support the VPMMA simply by purchasing your favorite goods and books on Amazon through their Smile portal!

About Russ Barnes, Colonel, USAF (ret), PhD, MBA, MS

Colonel, US Air Force (retired)

Dr. Russ Barnes is Chief Strategist for Systro Solutions, an organization development firm specializing in small business. He has more than 30 years' experience drawn from military service, small business ownership, executive coaching, strategy development and organization design consulting.

His Purposefully Profitable™ Program guides small business owners in creating and implementing a customized progression. In support of the Purposefully Profitable™ Program, he produced the Purposefully Profitable™ Podcast and the Mission Mapping™ Workshop. Russ speaks publicly on Organizing Your Business for Profitable Growth and CEO Skills for Small Business. He is the best-selling author of Small Business for Servicemembers: 15 Things You Need to Know to be Purposefully Profitable and a co-author of two best-selling books: Gamechangers for Government Contractors and Mission Unstoppable: Extraordinary Stories of Failures Blessings.

Dr. Barnes received his Bachelor in Business Administration from Manhattan College (NY), his Master in Business Administration (MBA) from Embry-Riddle Aeronautical University, his Master of Science in Strategic Studies from Air University, and his PhD in Organization Development from Benedictine University. The title of his dissertation is Organization Design for Small Business: A Discovery of Business Fundamentals for Executing a Purposeful Path to Profitability.

Connect with Russ by email - russ@systro.org or LinkedIn (www.linkedin.com/in/rcbarnes). For more information, visit www.systro.org.

About Jeremy Burdick, A&P, PMP, CMSgt Ret.

Jeremy is a United States Air Force (USAF) Veteran and a process specialist with more than 20 years of experience leading Project, Program, and Operational initiatives within large, diverse organizations. He has expertise in foreign affairs, policy analysis, instruction, training, and development. Jeremy entered the Air Force in 1996 as an Aircraft Propulsion Apprentice. He quickly rose from Apprentice through Journeyman to Craftsman while serving at both Dyess AFB, Texas and Yokota AB, Japan. Jeremy served as the NCOIC of Kit Section and Test Cell in the only Engine Regional Repair Center for the Pacific. He then decided to cross-train to Flight Engineer and he was once again assigned to both Dyess AFB, Texas then Yokota AB Japan, and finally Randolph AFB, Texas. He deployed several times throughout his career in support of many DoD campaigns including Joint Guard, Joint Forge, Provide Comfort, Southern Watch, Northern Watch, Enduring Freedom, Iraqi Freedom, etc. His final triple hatted position at Headquarters Air Education and Training Command was Major Command Functional Manager for enlisted aviators, Enlisted Aircrew Training Pipeline Manager, and Community College of the Air Force Accreditation Manager.

In 2018, Jeremy after retiring from the USAF, joined Vets2PM and served first, as a PMP Instructor, then quickly became the Operations Manager. Within the following year Jeremy became the Chief Operating Officer where he once again he serves his Veteran Brothers and Sisters around the globe.

Feel free to reach out to him at jeremy@vets2pm.com or visit **www.vets2pm.com**.

About Steven Crane, US Marine Corps Veteran

Steven Crane is a serial entrepreneur, mentor, and veteran advocate. As someone who experienced the stereotypical terrible military transition and lost everything, he now helps other veterans successfully transition from the service by providing them 360 degrees of care.

Steven brings a unique outlook to the transition process by blending proven industry principles, mental health counseling, and financial coaching all into a perfect marriage. He believes that if veterans have their wallets and minds taken care of, they can then focus on the firefight at hand, which is the transition process.

As a United States Marine Corps veteran, Steven understands the unique struggles of veterans transitioning into the civilian sector. When Steven is not assisting transitioning service members, he can be found writing or speaking on leadership topics such as change management, emotional intelligence, and finding purpose.

Steven lives to serve others and looks forward to serving you through your individual journey in living a more meaningful and fulfilled life!

Steven invites you to visit his website at:

www.stevencrane.com

About Paul DeJarnette, US Air Force Veteran

I am a Program Manager and problem solver at Amazon. Feel free to connect with me at:

https://www.linkedin.com/in/pdej7/

About Garrik Dennis

I'm a US Army veteran and currently serving the veteran community with Vets2PM as the lead instructor. I grew up and attended college in sunny southern California, then served for 8 years in the Infantry.

Upon my transition to the civilian lifestyle, I earned my PMP® certification through Vets2PM, joining the team soon after as an instructor. While an instructor, I was attending a graduate program for mental health counseling, which helped immensely in providing more personalized care for the veterans I was then reaching.

As the lead instructor now, it is my hope to bring more mental and emotional health services to the growing veteran community alongside the awesome Vets2PM team, as we attempt to help and inspire veterans to pursue meaningful, lucrative careers in the civilian marketplace.

My project experience ranges from small-unit tactical planning to brigade-level communications upgrades, and I have been instructing project management for multiple years. Although instructing is fun, I am truly passionate about assisting veterans in their pursuit in earning project management certifications, and in providing a streamlined transition process, however possible. I'm honored to have the opportunity to contribute to a book that aims to assist veterans, and it is my hope that it inspires others to pursue meaning, health, and a wonderful life.

About Reid Denson, PMP

Reid is a former U.S. Army Military Police officer who served in a variety of roles in Germany, Belgium, Iraq, Afghanistan, and within the U.S. Upon departure from active service in 2016, he used the professional equity he built as a military planner to obtain his certification and begin his civilian project management career, beginning with several years in the automotive manufacturing industry.

He is currently a Project Manager at Metabo HPT, a manufacturer of world-class power tools. At time of publication, Reid has nearly completed Master of Project Management degree from Western Carolina University. He resides in the greater Atlanta area with his wife Scarlett, son Thomas, and daughter Eva.

He is happy to connect with veterans and other aspiring PM's via Linked-In: https://www.linkedin.com/in/reid-denson/

About Joey Eisenzimmer, PMP

US Marine Corps Veteran

My career began professionally serving in the USMC from 2008-2013 on active duty as a Military Police Officer and eventually on a Special Reaction Team. After my EAS, I enrolled full time at a university in the Chicago area completing my undergraduate degree in business and then earning my MBA. Additionally, in 2015 I attended the Vets2PM PMP Boot Camp and passed the exam on my first attempt!

From there I entered the digital marketing and online space. I had the pleasure of working with and for Vets2PM at various points and it was an honor to continue serving our military veterans and their families. As my career progressed, I began gaining more technical skills and competencies and now work in the Cloud for Amazon Web Services. On the side, I continue as much as possible to keep sending the ladder back down to those transitioning from the service in the form of coaching/mentorship and volunteering.

Please feel free to reach out to me anytime via LinkedIn and we can connect further: https://www.linkedin.com/in/jeisenzimmer/ .

And remember, there are no obstacles, only opportunities!

About Dave Esra, PMP, ACP, Prosci Certified Change Practitioner

Dave is currently serving the United Services Automobile Association (USAA) Members as a PMO Leader for USAA Enterprise Compliance. He has worked as a Project Manager for the Department of Defense and the City of San Antonio in the Information Technology, Logistics, and Public Health spaces. Dave also held leadership positions in Risk and Compliance Management Programs for the DoD as a Uniformed Service Member as well as a Civilian.

Dave is a US Navy and US Army Veteran with over 20 years of service to our great nation. Currently, he is still serving as a US Army Reservist as an Inspector General in an Expeditionary Support Command. He has held multiple roles as an Infantry Officer, Civil Affairs Officer, and Logistician. Dave is especially honored to have received the General Douglas MacArthur award that is only given to the top five Junior Officers in the Army Reserves as well as the German Bronze Cross of Honor, the highest award a non-German Citizen can receive from the German Minister of Defense.

Dave has a MS in Executive Leadership from Grand Canyon University and a BS from Brenau University. He is a certified PMI Project Management Professional (PMP) and Agile Certified Practitioner (ACP). He is especially skilled at establishing standards and processes for Program Management Offices (PMOs) for large scale organizations.

Dave enjoys giving back to his military community by coaching and mentoring transitioning Service Members (or family members) who are interested in a career as a Project Manager. He can easily be contacted through the LinkedIn account listed.

LinkedIn: linkedin.com/in/daveesra

About Joshua P. Frank

Managing Partner, RSM Federal

Award-winning business coach, professional speaker, and bestselling author, Mr. Frank is a nationally recognized authority on government sales and business acceleration. With more than 30 years in the government space, he specializes in bridging government sales strategy with general business strategy. He is a recognized expert in the development and implementation of tactics and strategies required to differentiate, position for, and win government contracts. His training seminars are consistently rated as one of the strongest sessions at national conferences and events. Mr. Frank's coaching has helped companies win more than $2.7 Billion in definitive contracts and $30 billion in indefinite delivery contracts.

Managing Partner at RSM Federal, Mr. Frank is author of The Government Sales Manual; Amazon's #1 all-time GovCon bestseller An Insider's Guide to Winning Government Contracts – Real World Strategies, Lessons, and Recommendations; and Amazon's #1 bestseller Game Changers for Government Contractors. Mr. Frank received SBA's award for Veteran Business of the Year in addition to the National Award for Industry Small Business Advocate of the Year by the Society of American Military Engineers (SAME).

Visit www.authorjoshfrank.com to learn more.

Mr. Frank serves as Chairman of the Board for the Midwest Veterans Advocacy Foundation (VAF) / Veterans Business Resource Center (VBRC). Mr. Frank also supports the SBA's Emerging Leaders Program and judges applications for Arch Grants providing startup funding for entrepreneurs.

An avid outdoor enthusiast, Girl Scout and Boy Scout leader, Mr. Frank lives in St. Louis, Missouri with his wife, daughter, and son. He is a former military intelligence officer with an undergraduate degree in English, a Masters in Management Information Systems (MIS), and a Master's in Business Administration (MBA).

Feel free to contact Mr. Frank via LinkedIn.

https://www.linkedin.com/in/joshuapfrank

About Heide Gabriella

US Navy (Ret)

Heide Gabriella is a retired veteran with the US Navy where she gave her time as an air traffic controller. Now, Heide is an executive business coach, speaker, and entrepreneur.

Her transition to civilian life has given her great experiences that delivers powerful insights and passionate messages. From surviving bone cancer to becoming a mother of five, completing an Ironman, working as an engineer at NASA and navigating her career aspirations from her own intuition, Heide provides value, inspiration, and motivation to her audiences. She is here to serve and support veterans who are ready to create a life filled with passion and the freedom to live in their authenticity. She leads by example to inspire people to have courage, build confidence, realize that you are good enough, bring clarity to your purpose and guide you in a positive direction in business and life.

Heide has been featured in the media sharing her gifts and experiences that inspires the minds and hearts of her listeners. She has been featured in the Tampa Post, Chemo Buddies 4life and Women's Prosperity Network: The Unconference and WOW Wednesday. She graduated from Embry-Riddle Aeronautical University with a B.S. in Aerospace and retains the following credentials: John Maxwell Certified, Certified Master Practitioner NLP Coach, Certified Business Consultant, Certified Motivational Speaker and Founder of Veterans Leadership Conference.

Remember, you are not alone in this endeavor.

Visit me at https://www.heidegabriella.com and connect with me on LinkedIn http://linkedin.com/in/heidegabriella

About Clint Gershenson

Clint Gershenson is a Scrum Master and Agile Coach at Scaled Agile, Inc. Clint thrives at enhancing capabilities across teams by combining his expertise as an Agile coach at multiple technical companies with his experiences as a 10-year U.S. Army veteran.

Clint holds many of the top certifications around the world to include SAFe Program Consultant (SPC), Certified Scrum Professional, (CSP-SM), Lean Six Sigma Green Belt (LSSGB), Project Management Professional (PMP), PMI Agile Certified Practitioner (PMI-ACP), plus many more.

About Mark Giles, PMP, PMI-ACP, CISM

Mark was born in a small town in central Maine before enlisting in the United States Marine Corps in January 1988. After serving honorably for 6 years in the Marine Corps at Camp Foster, Okinawa, Japan and Marine Forces Atlantic, Norfolk, Virginia, he returned to his home state of Maine and enlisted in the Maine Air National Guard.

He was assigned to the 101st Communications Flight where he served as a Computer Systems Operator and later as an Infrastructure Technician. While assigned to the 101st Communications Flight, he was given, and accepted, opportunities to work multiple enterprise projects for the Air National Guard Readiness Center, Joint Base Andrews. After relocating to Joint Base Andrews, he served as an Information Technology Project Manager supporting the Air National Guard enterprise consisting of more than 250 locations around the world. He moved on to become the Base Communications Functional Area Manager before accepting his final assignment as the Cyber Planning, Integration & Sustainment Manager.

Mark retired from the United States Air Force and Air National Guard as a Chief Master Sergeant before accepting a position as a Program Manager for a Government contractor in the Washington D.C. area.

Contact Info: https://www.linkedin.com/in/mark-giles-pmp-pmi-acp-cism-39b630163/

About Mark Hannah, PMP, SA, CSM, SSGB, CBIP

Mark is currently CEO of Hannah Business Intelligence Solutions, Inc., a boutique independent consultancy with operations in Silicon Valley (CA). Marks journey began on the East Coast (N.C.) as an Enlisted Military kid. Shortly after his Marine father's retirement, he Enlisted in the Marines too and honorably served on Active Duty for ~12 years (1996 – 2007).

His initial MOS 3051 - Warehouse Clerk lasted four years, until he made a Lateral-move to MOS 0411 - Maintenance Mgt. Spec., as a "re-up" incentive - a tertiary MOS 0916 came later in his career. He served in all major USMC components: Division, FSSG, Wing, and HQ Base units, which provided an immense breadth of experience by the exposure to cross-functional/operational/inter-service functions. Moreover, chronological depth of experience gained in the Rank progression from Pvt to a SSgt. In the final contract, he both attended the Staff NCO Academy in parallel to online coursework at American Military University, earning an AA Degree.

At the Right Place & Time on a sensitive project, he collaborated with Grant Thornton Consultants at his unit, who mentored him with a Transition Roadmap. Post service, Mark worked as a Corporate Security Guard at Yahoo HQ, while simultaneously attending San Jose State University for a BSBA, concentrating in Management Information Systems – earning two Villanova University Master Certificates in Business Intelligence and Information Security.

He formed a thriving Veteran Student Organization while at SJSU and after graduation he immediately began contract consulting. A life-long learner, he is a self-taught Entrepreneur and enjoys the Startup, Cybersecurity, and Futurism scene. His Tech client portfolio consists of Adobe, Broadcom, Cisco, Hitachi, Microsoft, etc., consulting interns to CIOs. Having a unique proprietary skill set, toolbox, leadership style, and Startup sub-culture experience, Mark provides Project Management, Agile, and Entrepreneur instruction/coaching.

Email: mark@hannahbisolutions.com

LinkedIn: https://www.linkedin.com/in/markchannah/

About Kaylin Haywood

Certifications: Agile Fundamentals; Design Thinking, International Association of Innovation Professionals; Project Management Professional; Program Management Institute Innovation Professional; International Association of Innovation Professionals.
Consultant in Defense sector.

Accomplished 23-year Air Force officer (Ret) with experience in Space Control, Nuclear Weapons, Aircraft Depot Maintenance, and Planning, Programming, Budgeting, and Execution mission areas. Raised in Oklahoma and attended the University of Texas.

https://www.linkedin.com/in/kaylinhaywood

About Philip Hicks, PE, PMP

Phil is currently employed at DBi Services as Coastal District Vice President with branches in Baltimore MD, Chesapeake VA, Petersburg VA, Chesterfield VA, and Waynesboro VA. DBi Services provides infrastructure maintenance, operations and management solutions in North America for government agencies, utilities, private industries, railways, retailers and other infrastructure owners. He is responsible for the overall business performance and growth of his District, providing a variety of services with a fleet of over 130 trucks/equipment and over 135 teammates.

Phil developed his passion for helping veterans as he went through trials and tribulations during his transition from the Air Force in 2014. Phil has volunteered time with American Corporate Partners (ACP) as a volunteer advisor since 2014, Veterati as a mentor since 2015, the Society of American Military Engineers (SAME) as the Emergency Preparedness Committee Chair since 2019.

He has also offered time to the Veteran Project Manager Mentoring Alliance (VPMMA) since its founding in 2020 as a member of the board of directors serving as Treasurer, lead for Professional Services, and most recently was elected as President. Phil has been married to Monica for 22 years and has three children, Candace – 29, Daniel – 17, and Samuel 15.

LinkedIn: https://www.linkedin.com/in/philhicks1

See contact info at LinkedIn for phone number and personal e-mail address.

About Craig A. Jones, USMC Ret. PMP/PMI-ACP

Craig retired from the United States Marine Corps in 2010 following his service during Operation Iraqi Freedom that resulted in extensive combat wounds. Along with the award of the Purple Heart, Craig also earned the Navy and Marine Corps Achievement Medal with a combat distinguishing device among his many unit and individual awards. Craig began his civilian career in the public safety sector where he led operations, programs, and projects in support of emergency first responders.

Presently, Craig is a Program & Project Manager that leads key strategic IT development initiatives as the product owner for a Fortune 100 financial services company, along with leading their veteran's employee resource group for the Phoenix Region. Additionally, Craig is the Founder of & Chief Consultant/Lead Instructor for Veteran Consulting LLC, a Member of the Board of Directors (Professional Services) & mentor for a National non-profit, Veteran Project Management Mentor Alliance (VPMMA), and a mentor and career counselor on several other platforms assisting service members and military spouses transition into the next chapter and into project management.

He holds a Master's degree in Personal Financial Planning, a Bachelor's degree in Operations Management, and is certified as a Project Management Professional (PMP), Agile Certified Practitioner (ACP), in Change Management, and as a SAFe Agilist.

A native of Ohio, Craig moved to Arizona with his family as a child and made it his home. Together with his wife, he is raising two children in the city of Phoenix.

About Daniel Kaminske, US Air Force Veteran, EE, MBA, CSM, PMP

I am a technical project manager and engineering leader with 10+ years of experience in engineering and operations management. An advocate for business process development and continuous improvement in efficiency, I enjoy helping organizations improve processes and achieve their strategic goals. As a natural communicator I am an essential team manager, product, and process engineer with a keen focus on integration of current business improvement methodologies and industry tools to streamline design, manufacturing, and operational processes.

Outside of work, I enjoy playing guitar, running, and cycling, rock climbing, and modifying
cars and other improvement projects.

Feel free to reach out to me by email at
dankaminske@gmail.com

About Mike Klingshirn, MPH, CPH, PMP

Mike is board certified in Public Health, with a concentration in epidemiology and biostatistics. He earned his Bachelor of Science in Pharmaceutical Sciences from the University of Toledo and his Master of Public Health from the University of South Florida.

Mike has held multiple roles as an Air Force Officer. He has led the Public Health efforts at Fairchild AFB, Shaw AFB, Air Force's Central Command, and Task Force South East (renamed Task Force COVID), to include deployments to Camp Lemonier, Djibouti and Al Udeid AB, Qatar.

Mike earned his CPH certification in 2011 and his PMP in 2019. He has transitioned into the Director of Consulting Services role at Fusion Cell, a company bringing military talent into civilian corporations.

You can contact him at:
mklingshirn@fusioncell.com
or www.LinkedIn.com/in/michael-klingshirn

About Kevin A. Knight

I didn't know about project management until my last deployment in 2016 when my lieutenant mentioned it to me. He explained to me I have essentially been managing projects for the Army for the past 6 years and didn't even realize it. That was my starting point to getting into project management and led me to where I am today.

During that deployment, I began studying and reading the PMBOK Guide and signed up for a class with Vets2PM. Once I returned home, I enrolled into DeVry College of New York and obtained my Bachelors of Technical Management with a focus in project management at the end of 2018. I also have an Associates of Architectural Engineering and an Associates of Electrical and Electronics Engineering

I started managing projects in the civilian workforce while attending college in 2017 for a telematics installations company. Currently I am with a global pharmaceutical company as an IT infrastructure project manager located in south-central Pennsylvania.

What I like most about project management is working through problems and collaborating with colleagues to resolve those problems as effectively as possible. I also enjoy the opportunity project management offers to continually learn new and enhance my skills, approaches, techniques, and tactics. This provides the ability for me to build on my project management skills and become a more effective project manager. While I have only been a project manager or a few years, I am looking forward to the skills and experiences it offers me in the coming years.

Feel free to reach out and connect with me anytime on LinkedIn at https://www.linkedin.com/in/KevinA-Knight/

About Matthew Kolakowski

Matthew Kolakowski is an executive and scholarly academic with over 14 years of experience in leading health care facilities for organizations with up to 3,000 employees. Expertise with health care project management, organizational leadership, and operations management to drive patient-centered care outcomes. He has managed over 65 people responsible for health care operations, training, cross-cultural engagement, and regulatory compliance with personnel spanned across the globe. His approach to health care operations, project management, and his academic roles focus on collaboration, trust-building, reinforcement of core competencies, and establishing confidence.

He completed his Ph.D. in Business Administration at Oklahoma State University. His research focuses include healthcare leadership traits and the psychological characteristics of entrepreneurs that impact entrepreneurial venture performance.

About Michael LeJeune

Michael LeJeune is a bestselling author and master coach with RSM Federal. Michael hosts the wildly popular Govcon podcast **Game Changers for Government Contractors**, manages the **Federal Access Knowledge-Base** and training platform, and specializes in helping Govcon business owners brand themselves as Subject Matter Experts in their niche.

Michael and his business partner Joshua Frank have helped their Govcon clients win over $2.6 billion in government contracts since 2008. Over 1,000 Government contractors trust the Federal Access Knowledge-Base as their primary source of Govcon education, training, coaching, and practical strategies for winning government contracts.

Register your free Federal-Access account today by visiting: https://federal-access.com/join/

About Timothy R McCardle, PMP, Six Sigma Black Belt

Timothy served 26 years as an active duty US Marine retiring as a Master Gunnery Sergeant (E-9). He served in numerous billets in Marine Aviation and as an Embassy Security Guard.

In Tim's post-military career, he has worked as a Continuous Improvement professional in three different industries. He is currently working as contractor logistics support to Naval Aviation Support Equipment program.

Contact information: https://www.linkedin.com/in/tim-mccardle-84a9a313/

About James C. McCulley Jr, PMP

ARMY SFC Retired; AA-Applied Science -Technology Troubleshooting

Combat Army Veteran of 21 years now working as an Assistant Project Manager for an Electrical contractor. After retiring from the Army as an M1 Abrams Tank Systems Maintainer, I didn't know what I was going to do next. Leading troops and running motor pools was all I knew. Besides the coveted DA Civilian jobs that require someone to either retire or die before you can get in, what else could I do?

Turns out everything I was doing in the military was Project Management. Thanks to the Vets2PM team, I was able to make a smooth transition into the field. The presence of the PMP certification opened the door for new opportunities. Without that credential I wouldn't have the job I do.

Now I am a successful member of the Project Management team with Miller-Lighthouse LLC in Richmond, VA working on a massive data center for a worldwide client.

About Cathy Miclat

Professional Resume Writer & Career Services Expert

I am the daughter of a US Army Reserve Veteran and have nearly 30 years of experience in Human Resources and Executive search. After graduating with a BS in Mass Communications and spending time in Advertising in Missouri and Virginia, I switched gears and became a recruiter for an executive search firm. After moving to the Hampton Roads, VA area, I spent four years as a Human Resources Manager with a small government contractor where I managed the recruitment processes during a time that we doubled in size, and ensured EEO compliance for diversity hiring. Relocating to Northern Virginia in 2000 led to an 18-year tenure with an executive search firm, where I placed candidates in technical and leadership roles.

To satisfy my love of writing and expand on my desire to help people achieve meaningful, lucrative careers, I became a Professional Resume writer. I helped a struggling Veteran with his resume, and it turned around his job search, earning him multiple interviews while changing the trajectory of his then current situation. We remain good friends to this day and he introduced me to Vets2PM – where I found my true passion.

Today, I am the Director of Career Services with Vets2PM where I build upon each client's professional experience and industry credentials to assist with professional resume writing, career placement, and job search strategies. I work with recruiters and talent acquisition professionals at organizations that are committed to diversifying their workforce through subscriptions to PurpleX, our cultivated candidate database, job posting services, flat fee placement services, PMaaS, and Corporate Partnerships, where I am able to bridge the gap between Veteran underemployment *and* Corporate America's ability to identify and hire qualified Veteran talent.

Feel free to reach out to me at:
Cathy@Vets2PM.com

About Raphael Montgomery, PMP, PMI-ACP, CSM

Raphael retired from the United States Army in March of 2020 after 25 years of service, where he had the opportunity to lead multiple teams and organizations and manage multimillion programs. He is currently employed by USAA as a Senior Program / Project Manager, where he a leads compliance related projects.

Contact information: linkedin.com/in/raphael-brian-montgomery

About Misty Moreno, Air Force Veteran

Misty joined the military at the age of 21 and is a Human Resources professional.

Misty has been married to Johnie for 15 years and has a 13-year-old son. Misty and Johnie both retired from the Air Force on September 1, 2020.

The Moreno family resides in South Carolina and Misty is a Human Relations Business Partner at Sumter Continental Tire Plant.

About James Onder

James Onder grew up an only child to a single mother in Bangor, Maine. Life challenged him at a very early age, from multiple moves, to living on welfare and food stamps, and in government housing. At 20 years old, he found himself broke, working dead end jobs, and a high school dropout. Thinking that there had to be more to life, he finished high school and joined the Air Force.

The Air Force afforded him an opportunity to learn a trade in the HVAC career field. The Air Force also afforded him the opportunity to travel the world. He was stationed in Germany twice, Italy, Guam, Hawaii, Japan, and Korea. Another opportunity he was afforded that he once thought impossible, was college. He completed his Associates Degree in Electrical and Mechanical Technologies through the Community College of the Air Force, and went on to get a Bachelor's Degree in Business Administration, Human Resource Management from Columbia Southern University graduating Magna cum Laude.

Prior to retiring after 26 years of service, he attended a Project Management Professional (PMP) boot camp through Vets2PM, and six months later obtained his PMP. He resides in Colorado Springs with his wife Erica, and two sons Tyler and Ryley. He currently works as a defense contractor for United States Space Command, consulting on the standup of the United States' newest combatant command.

When not working and spending time with family, he enjoys telling his story of how he got to where he is, and his transition story to soon-to-be retired or separated service members. He feels we can all learn something every day, and believes "If you're not learning, you're not living".

About Eric Paddock

CMSgt(ret)

Eric Paddock served 25 years in the Air Force and held strategic positions as a Major Command Functional Manager for AFCENT, Europe and Africa. He spent three years attached to a Special Operations unit as a Combat Airspace Manager, and his final position was as an Operations Group Superintendent overseeing 1.2K personnel across three countries.

He is led large scale projects impacting international relations across the globe and he is embedded within the U.S. Secret Service overseeing projects directly impacting the President of the United States. After leaving the military, Eric was a Project Management instructor assisting military personnel achieve their PMP goals and now serves as a military liaison for Colorado Christian University.

Contact: https://www.linkedin.com/in/ericspaddock

About Patrick Pressoir, MSc, PMP

Patrick is a veteran of the Canadian Armed Forces Air Defence Artillery. He transitioned to the private sector after having worked in the Directorate of Land Requirements on equipment acquisition projects for the army of the future.

With a bachelor's degree in Business Administration and a Masters in Management Science, Patrick went on to specialize in the fields of continuous improvement, project management and change management creating unique skillset mix that allows him to help organizations plan, execute and successfully navigate through major transformational change.

Connect with Patrick on LinkedIn at http://linkedin.com/in/patrickpressoir

About Joe Pusz

"PMO Joe"

Joe Pusz is a Veterans Advocate, Author, Speaker, Entrepreneur, and global leader in the PMO and Project Management Community. He has been recognized for his efforts and listed as one of the Top 15 PMO Influencers in the World by the PMO Global Alliance.

Joe is Co-Founder of VPMMA, the Veteran Project Manager Mentor Alliance which is a 501c3 Non-Profit Organization assisting Veterans seeking to transition into civilian Project Management careers.

VPMMA has greater than 400 participants including members from all branches of the military. VPMMA provides Veterans and Spouses individual mentoring and professional services through existing partnerships with Arizona State University, Freeport McMoRan, International Institute for Learning, PMI-Phoenix, Sensei Project Solutions, Silicon Valley Bank, THE PMO SQUAD, and Vets2PM.

Joe is Founder and President of THE PMO SQUAD, a Phoenix based PMO and Project Management Consulting firm. For over 7 years THE PMO SQUAD has been helping clients build and implement PMOs and providing PM resources to lead strategic client projects. THE PMO SQUAD is home of the Purpose Driven PMO methodology helping PMO leaders establish successful long-term PMOs by starting with Purpose.

He is host of the Project Management Office Hours Radio Show and Podcast providing Project Management Leaders a voice within our community. The show is in their 3rd season and is the #1 live Project Management show in the United States. They have hosted over 100 National and International guests. To date the show has over 20 million plays and downloads with 33% of their global audience from international listeners.

www.thevpmma.org

www.thepmosquad.com

www.projectmanagementofficehours.com

https://www.linkedin.com/in/joepusz/

About Ray K. Ragan, MAd (PM), PMP

Ray is the Co-Founder of Clear Core and helps Credit Unions use data strategically. Prior to Clear Core, Ray worked in defense and financial technology, bringing machine learning, intelligence systems, and speech analytics to enterprise scale.

Ray studied strategy and risk at Stanford University and the U.S. Army Command and General Staff College. Ray holds a Master's degree in Administration from Northern Arizona University and is a credentialed Project Management Profession (PMP) with several Agile certifications.

Ray is a combat veteran and a highly decorated U.S. Army Reserve officer currently leading the U.S. Army Innovation Command's Arizona Team.

About Adam Reed

As a retiring 20-year Navy Aviator and veteran with over 2,000 flight hours in the P3-C Orion aircraft and having been stationed and deployed around the world, I would say my time spent in Scotland was the most enjoyable of them all.

During these last 20 years the Navy has allowed me an opportunity to obtain both, an undergraduate and graduate degree along with multiple other professional certifications. As a certified Project Manager Professional and Lean Six Sigma Black Belt I have spent the last decade leading executive initiatives and delivering results.

In August of 2019, I started my transition journey from Sailor to Civilian. It has been difficult to say the least and filled with uncertainty and anxiety. I learned that my struggles were not my own and others that have made the transition have experienced them too. I have learned from others and feel that it's our duty to pass on what we have learned to those who follow in our path. I knew what I wanted and worked as hard as I had to, to achieve my goal. I will begin my next career at Amazon but my passion is to share my experiences so others can have a successful transition experience as well.

As my military career has come to an end, the desire to help fellow veterans has only begun. If you have any questions about my transition or would like to connect with me, please connect with me on LinkedIn at

https://www.linkedin.com/in/adamtreedpmp/

About Nick Roberge, PMP, Capt USMC (ret)

Nick Roberge is a retired Marine Corps Aircraft Maintenance Officer and current business owner. His early days in the Corps included troubleshooting and repairing avionics systems on H-1 helicopters. He received a commission through the Enlisted Commissioning Program and transitioned to managing maintenance teams for C-130Js. Nick reconnected with his earlier passion for competitive shooting and went on the lead the USMC Shooting Team as his final tour.

After retiring in 2015 and experiencing a longer than expected transition period, Nick discovered Vets2PM and attained his PMP certification shortly afterwards. He was quickly hired by a government contracting firm and was able to put his expertise and newly attained credentials to use immediately. Nick spent a few years assisting program managers within multiple scientific fields, providing training to active duty members, and performing various duties as a systems analyst.

Nick wanted to expand his horizons and eventually become an independent business owner but did not know how to go about it. He had learned of and later been accepted to the Entrepreneurial Boot Camp for Veterans (EBV) program through IMVF and Syracuse University and graduated with his cohort in early 2019. The following week he founded "Begunners" and continued his passion for teaching marksmanship while learning how to run a business. Soon afterwards another opportunity came along to enter the roof restoration industry, where his background in maintenance, scheduling, and project management propelled him further as a successful business owner.

Nick currently resides with his family in Fredericksburg, VA, cheers on his Boston based sports teams, and continues his involvement within various shooting sports. "I cannot thank Vets2PM and the IMVF folks running the EBV program enough for helping me to get to where I am today and where I plan to be in the exciting years ahead".

About Stuart Smith

Stuart is experienced leading and supporting large-scale strategic initiatives, helping organizations both install and realize the benefits of quality systems management, customer relationship management, enterprise technology systems, organization design efforts and leadership development.

He has studied strategy execution over the past twenty-five years. He is a past national member of the Association of Strategic Planning and has facilitated or co-facilitated thirty comprehensive and specific-focus strategic planning sessions (innovation to market segmentation) for business, government, and not-for-profit clients. He brings the best in recognized planning processes to bear, while developing organizational capacity.

He has over thirty years' experience with thousands of hours delivering in-person training sessions in leadership, communication, decision-making, resource and project management, quality program management. He has designed and facilitated +500 in-person and virtual meetings, work sessions, off-sites, and retreats to develop plans, solve problems address conflict, build teams, and lead change. He began facilitating small-group leadership programs in US Army leadership schools.

Business, Community and Veteran Leader: Stuart is a past Board Member of the Atlanta Society for Human Resource Management (SHRM) and SHRM National; previous member of the International Association of Facilitators and the Association of Strategic Planners (ASP) and the American Society for Quality.

He is a former Rotarian and lives by the Rotary Motto *"Service Above Self"*. He is a Paul Harris Fellow, has been awarded the Pat Adkins "Rotarian of the Year" award.

He is a distinguished US Army Veteran and was recognized by the 9th Infantry Division, I Corp and FORSCOM as the 1988 Soldier of the Year. He now focuses his volunteer efforts on Veterans' advocacy in employment and entrepreneurship. He has led the Military Affairs Council of the Cocoa Beach Regional Chamber of Commerce and is a founding board member of the Florida Association of Veteran Owned Businesses – Space Coast Chapter. He is a member of the Disabled American Veterans, American Legion, and life member of the Brevard County Veterans Center.

Stuart is a 2018 Inductee into the Space Coast Public Service Hall of Fame, Outstanding Military Service Award, Brevard County, FL

Stuart earned his Bachelor of Science in Workforce Education from Southern Illinois University (Carbondale) and a Master of Education, HR Concentration from Seattle University. He is a life-long learner and student of Dr. Edwards Deming's Quality Leadership Philosophy. He has an in-depth understanding of Systems Theory and how people work most effectively in organizations.

He has developed his facilitation skills earning recognition in the field and has held the following professional facilitation certifications:
Certified Master Facilitator (**CMF**), *International Institute for Facilitation*
Certified Professional Facilitator (**CPF**), *International Association of Facilitators*
Stuart is also a well-rounded business leader and has mastered the body of knowledge and held the following professional certifications:
Senior Professional of Human Resources (**SPHR**), *Society for Human Resource Management,* 2008-2012
Certified Manager of Quality and Organizational Excellence (**CMQOE**) and Senior Manager, *American Society for Quality*, 2004-2012
Trained Six Sigma Black and Green Belt, *Georgia Tech* 2002

<u>Trained Change Management Practitioner</u>, 2000 *Conner and Associates*

Stuart's contact information is:

321-313-5325
theprofessionalfacilitator@gmail.com
http://www.linkedin.com/pub/stuart-smith/0/a06/634

About Bruce Townshend

Bruce Townshend is a retired Army and Army Reserve Military Police and Public Affairs Officer with 28 years of combined service. During his career he had assignments to many posts in the United States and overseas to Panama, Germany, Korea and a deployment to Kuwait and Iraq in 2003 for Operation Iraqi Freedom. A native of Lowell, MA he enlisted in 1981 and finished his military career in 2011 with the rank of Major. He is a 1987 graduate of Northeastern University with a degree in Criminal Justice and Law Enforcement. Bruce currently works for the Department of Defense as the chief of employer outreach for Employer Support of the Guard and Reserve (ESGR) and is on the Private and Public Engagement team for the Defense Personnel and Family Support Center (DPFSC) in Alexandria, VA. He has devoted his career to serving Veterans and their families, traveling all around the country every year. He is proud to say that he has visited all 50 states. He is currently pursuing his PMP certification.

Bruce's LinkedIn profile is: https://www.linkedin.com/in/bruce-townshend-658b4113/. He can also be found on YouTube at BT's Corner.

Bruce has three grown children and six grandchildren. He currently resides in Virginia's Shenandoah Valley with his soon-to-be wife, Robin. He likes to play poker, homebrew beer, and write. He is learning to play the bagpipes, which is why he lives deep in the woods.

About Robert K. Tyson MBA, PMP, CSM, CSPO, TS-SCI

Mr. Robert Tyson retired from 25 years of US Army service, having spent most of his career in Special Forces and Special Missions. He has worked in a combination of full-time employment and consulting where he gained expertise in Technology Management, Program Management, Business Development and Business Process Improvement. Beginning with his service in Special Forces and culminating with a business education focused on technology, entrepreneurship, and commercialization, he developed a keen sense for identifying opportunity as it relates to risk, requirements, people, integration, and validation.

His background has taught him to build capacity in others while his education has empowered him to optimize and focus those efforts regardless of their physical or technological attributes. He now possesses a unique and natural ability to determine business requirements based on personal engagements and data analysis.

While his professional sites are set on growth within a large corporation, his personal goal is to grow his entrepreneurial partnership, The Gideon Group (WOSB/SDVOSB), into a fulfilling and profitable organization where fellow SOF retirees and other veterans can work and share in the profits based on personally invested effort in their own futures. His inspiration comes from engaging and working with like-minded entrepreneurs who set lofty goals for themselves while providing valuable technical services to the community and the nation.

In a continued thirst for knowledge and capacity Mr. Tyson begins a Juris Doctorate (JD) program this fall, 2020. When complete, he hopes to work as corporate counsel for a large enterprise while also serving The Gideon Group with his new skill set.

Robert is married to Gretchen Tyson and they have three delightful daughters together: Heather, Summer, and Ella. They are an outdoors family and supportive of Robert's passion for hunting in his spare time during the winter months.

About Carlos Victor Ulibarri, PMP

Albuquerque, NM

US Air Force (2014-2020); Osan, Korea (2016-2017); Spangdahlem, Germany (2017-2020)

I was a high school dropout at 17 years old. I managed to convince my parents, both educators at the time, to allow me to stop going to school and get my GED and EMT license from a local community college. I spent my early 20s serving my community in Albuquerque, NM, where I responded to numerous 911 calls. I was able to help many people.

To take my skills to the next level, I joined the Air Force with the goal of working in special operations. After months of intense training, I failed. I decided to remain in the Air Force and see out my contract as an engineering technician. I regret nothing; my years of service have allowed me to see the world and expand my skillset in a way I had not considered. I have become a person who is sought out by leaders to solve problems, improve processes, and make their decisions a little easier. This experience has taught me to remain open to multiple possibilities and always keep moving forward.

https://www.linkedin.com/in/carlos-victor-ulibarri/

About Craig Washburn, CEO, VTC Veteran Tax Credits, Veteran, USN

Craig Washburn is the founder and CEO of VTC Veteran Tax Credits. Craig's passion to help his fellow servicemembers began shortly after high school.

On Jan 03, 1991, just a month before the start of the first Gulf War, Craig joined the United States Navy. He served two years attached to Helicopter Anti-Submarine Squadron Light Four Zero then two years deployed on the USS Saratoga (CV-60).

After four years of active duty, Petty Officer Second Class Washburn returned to the civilian world and completed his Bachelor of Science in Information Technology from the University of Central Florida. Since then, Craig has held several leadership roles in the financial and insurance industries before opening his first company, in 2007.

This is when Craig found another passion, helping businesses. In this role, Craig helped businesses regain control of their Human Resources budget through tailored strategic solutions. In 2016, Craig saw an opportunity to create a solution to help both Veterans and businesses better leverage a decades old Department of Labor Program, that rewards businesses for hiring Veterans. It was the perfect opportunity to marry both passions and give back to the communities that have given him so much.

After two and a half years of research and development, Craig built the www.veteranstaxcredits.com platform and founded VTC Veteran Tax Credits. The mission of the program is to make it easier for Veterans transition into their next careers and easier for companies to generate additional revenue that can be allocated toward future Veteran hiring initiatives.

About Dana L. White

Founder / CEO JDOTMedia.com

Entrepreneur, Business Owner, and Air Force reservist Dana L. White is a visionary, motivator, and philanthropist. In the Air Force Reserves, Dana is a SF/Combat Arms Instructor for the Pararescuemen, a Combat Search and Rescue Unit. He comes from a military family and as a 10-year Veteran, service to others is in Dana's DNA. Not only does he embody the adage of "where there is a will, there is a way", but Dana is also passionate about giving back to the community, especially supporting education. His creativity and perseverance have enabled him to overcome obstacles, challenges, and setbacks. As a result, he also helps others by sharing his creativity, stories of triumph and the lessons that he has learned.

As a civilian, despite the accolades, life has always presented challenges in the form of the less than ideal family life with substance abuse and lack of stability. These obstacles instilled an unyielding drive in Dana to overcome the circumstances that he was born into and to make generational changes for his two daughters, Trinity and Judea. At the age of 18, when the NBA was no longer a reality, he focused on his lifelong dream of becoming a Mechanical Engineer. After completing vocational education, Dana secured his first engineering job as a drafter/designer. From there, his career spanned over 15 years of experience in Mechanical, Land Development, Forensic and Architectural Engineering. Eventually, Dana started his own drafting and design firm which he ran for several years prior to starting his military career.

Dana continues to harness his many talents as he transitions from his military career. He works with other entrepreneurs to grow their businesses through his digital marketing agency, JDOT Media® to help businesses "Create their identity, define their services, and brand their businesses". Dana is also starting a project called "One Real Story™" to help others share their journey.

About Eric "Doc" Wright, PhD

My own transition from military-to-project manager-to-corporate America took twelve, long, dark, agonizing years. In fact, it almost killed me!

However, once in business, my 20+ year ascension to success has been consistent; student-to-salesman-to-project manager-to-government accountant and project officer-to-professor-to-founder of Vets2PM, LLC (www.vets2pm.com) and its PDU University (www.pduuniversity.com), and Co-Founder of the 501(c)3 Veteran Project Manager Mentor Alliance (www.thevpmma.org).

I now use my pain, my organizations, the books I contribute to, and my deep knowledge of how corporate America works to help other military veterans achieve meaningful, lucrative post-service intra or entrepreneur careers too.

Additionally, during my civil service at DOD, I paid vendors, received goods and services from them, and performed as the government's Contracting Officer Representative ("COR") on an IT system development and deployment project. I use that experience too to consult government on statutory staff training and credentialing to increase compliance and retention; and to coach other small veteran-owned businesses ("VOB") to increased profitability, productivity, and performance!

I have found through helping thousands of military veterans achieve careers with purpose, meaning, challenging work, and nice paycheck, these things can take a lot of pressure off other areas of the transition, and life.

My additional areas of interest are: (1) Decision-making and behavior under time, risk, and uncertainty; (2) Exploring the motivation, pay, and performance equation, and (3) Helping small companies achieve the profitability, productivity, and performance of larger companies, without the larger staff carrying costs.

I am at:
1. www.calendly.com/docwright for phone calls.
2. eric@vets2pm.com for emails, keynote speaking inquiries, and business conversations about how we help government agencies at all levels.

3. https://rsmfederal.com/government-consulting-services for business coaching.
4. And www.linkedin.com/docwright for connections.

Made in the USA
Monee, IL
29 September 2021

79053490R00173